THE REAL READER'

Slightly Foxed

'Tusker's Last Stand'

NO.9 SPRING 2006

Publisher and co-editor Gail Pirkis
Co-editor Hazel Wood
Marketing Kathleen Smith
Publicity Stephanie Allen

Cover illustration by Emma McClure
Emma McClure trained as a painter at Winchester and Chelsea Schools of Art and now lives and works in London. She exhibits regularly and has had several successful one-person exhibitions at the Cadogan Contemporary Gallery. She can be contacted on: 07748 408937 or emmamcclure@hotmail.com.

Design by Octavius Murray

Colophon and tailpiece by David Eccles

Published by Slightly Foxed Limited
67 Dickinson Court
15 Brewhouse Yard
London ECIV 4JX

tel 020 7549 2121/2111
fax 0870 1991245
e-mail all@foxedquarterly.com
www.foxedquarterly.com

Annual subscription rates (4 issues)
UK £32; Europe £37; Rest of the World £42
Single copies can be bought for £8 (UK) or £10 (overseas)
Back issues are also available

ISBN 0-9551987-0-4
ISBN 978-0-9551987-0-0

Printed and bound by Smith Settle, Otley

Contents

Illustration by Clifford Harper, from E. H. Gombrich, *A Little History of the World* (see p.61)

From the Editors

When we mentioned last year that we were moving to a new office, with spectacular views over St Paul's, we're not sure what image this will have conjured up. One of those atmospheric, old-fashioned magazine offices perhaps, heaped with books and unread submissions, where coffee was made with a kettle rather than a machine and the switchboard was manned by a chirpy character who'd been there for decades, recognized callers' voices and always knew where everyone was.

In some respects this isn't so inaccurate. When we started *Slightly Foxed* – having had a brief taste of the corporate world – we knew we wanted a set-up where a real person answered the phone, where we didn't spend all our time 'in meetings' and where 'over-30' wasn't necessarily a term of abuse. 'Small is beautiful' was our watchword, and now, with the confidence of two happy, even flourishing, years behind us, we feel it may be time to reveal just how small.

In fact, the core staff of *Slightly Foxed* numbers three, all of us part-time. Behind us hovers a stalwart back-up team who come in on an ad hoc basis to help with marketing, sort out the computers and man the office in times of emergency. This is sometimes augmented by other helpful people on work experience who do the filing, stuff envelopes, go to the bank and the post office and generally make themselves useful – one of them, Patrick Evans, contributed an excellent piece to Issue 5 on *The Leaping Hare*. Husbands and children pitch in loyally when required and, of course, Pugwash the cocker spaniel also makes his own special contribution by forcing us out into the fresh air occasionally.

Backing us all up is a group of equally important and supportive people – our investors. There is nothing corporate about them either: they are all friends who were generous enough to chance some of their own money on setting up this new venture, and without them we would never have got off the ground. And we mustn't forget to mention our kindly accountant, who travels up from Gloucestershire to give us encouragement and sage advice, and the other members of our Board who gather round the kitchen table a couple of times a year to do the same.

Small though we are, we do have many years' experience in publishing and journalism between us and aim to do things professionally while – we hope – providing cheer and entertainment, which is our primary concern. We've been saddened to see how, in the world of corporate publishing, editorial has become synonymous with marketing (the only important question about a potential book being 'Will Waterstones take it?') and standards of editing have dropped.

But looking on the bright side, there are still some good editors left, as demonstrated by Charles Elliott's piece on p.84. And if this stimulates your interest in the relationship between writer and editor, do read Diana Athill's *Stet*, about her time working for the publisher André Deutsch, or Gardner Bottsford's recently published *A Life of Privilege, Mostly*, by a contributor to the *New Yorker* in the days of the fabled editor William Shawn.

We certainly feel we have a life of privilege producing *Slightly Foxed*, since dealing with you all, subscribers and contributors alike, has turned out to be pure pleasure. We look forward to hearing from you this year – even during evenings and weekends, which is not unusual! – and would be delighted, in particular, to know your reactions to our Christmas stocking-filler *Ghost Writer*, which so many of you loyally bought.

GAIL PIRKIS
HAZEL WOOD

Tusker's Last Stand

ANNABEL WALKER

Mussoorie, India, 1990: Tibetan guest-house canteen meals have had an unfortunate effect on my digestive system and several more weeks of turbulence lie in prospect before I leave. The only food available from the nearby shop is packeted biscuits and salted peanuts, the latter sold in paper cones made of discarded test sheets from the government college opposite. I consider myself fairly practical about food but even I prefer not to contemplate two months of nothing but custard creams. So I take a walk along the wooded track towards the town and call at the Carlton Hotel.

Fortunately, in 1990 I hadn't yet encountered Paul Scott's novel *Staying On* (though it should have been essential preparatory reading for a visit to a hill station). If I had, my delight in discovering the Carlton might have been diluted by unavoidable comparisons and time-wasting attempts to identify its role as a model for Smith's, the hotel in the novel. Instead, I happily immersed myself in its frayed colonial charm for a few hours each weekend, eating lunch alone at a dining-table large enough to seat twelve and retiring afterwards to a cane chair on the enclosed veranda that ran along one side of the building. There were rarely other guests.

The Carlton, like the fictional Smith's Hotel, was a relic of British rule in India and of the British taste for life in the Himalayan foothills. The damp mountain climate and limited business had left it a little dilapidated but, in common with Scott's female protagonist

---

Paul Scott, *Staying On* (1977)
Arrow · Pb · 258pp · £7.99 · ISBN 0099443198

in the novel, Lucy Smalley, it kept up appearances and retained its dignity. Smith's, by contrast, is seedy, unkempt and owned by a scheming egotist, Mrs Bhoolaboy, who is concerned not with her hotel's character or even its viability, but with its value as a redevelopment site. Many poignant moments in the novel arise as a result of the cultural chasm that lies between Mrs Bhoolaboy and her tenants, the Smalleys, the British couple who are 'staying on'.

Frayed colonial charm: Central Hotel, Simla

Tusker and Lucy Smalley are remnants of the fictional world of Scott's famous *Raj Quartet*. While acquaintances such as the Laytons return to England at Independence in 1947, the Smalleys move only from the military to the civilian world, opting for life as 'boxwallahs' in India rather than one of drab penury back home. Their retirement visit to the hill station of Pankot turns into permanent residence in the lodge at Smith's Hotel, and it is here that the novel is set, during the last three months of Tusker's life in early 1972.

Despite the apparent confines of the setting, the reader may well lose track of time. Scott is meticulous about the chronology, but the dates he provides are densely interspersed with the minutiae of the Smalleys' lives, past and present, as well as those of the secondary characters, in the form of their own unspoken reflections and memories. Thus a chapter that begins on a Monday morning in 1972 and moves no further forward than lunchtime may, through the apparently unedited private thoughts of Lucy, for example, range back to 1925 and end in 1947, flowing unchecked through the personal experiences that form her view of life.

For this reason alone, the book is best read at a sitting or two when you can allow yourself to be carried along on the streams of consciousness of the various characters. There is Lucy Smalley, almost permanently adrift in the past, both real and imagined; the hapless Mr Bhoolaboy, in thrall to his ghastly wife; and the incomparable Ibrahim, Tusker Smalley's bearer, who takes a respectful but dispassionate interest in his impoverished employers and has learned to play a good-humoured minor role in the tortured game of manners by which they communicate with each other.

Alternatively, you can force yourself to be a little more objective and admire Scott's discreetly controlling hand as he tells a story that is both richly comic and terribly sad. Gradually revealing more and more detail via thoughts and conversations, he lays bare the complex, inarticulate relationship between Tusker and Lucy and prompts tears as easily with humour as with poignancy. The farcical activities of the Bhoolaboys are particularly enjoyable, as in the chapter in which Mr Bhoolaboy tries to reconcile his religious impulses with his carnal desires, with its detailed description of his escape from the clutches of his sleeping wife:

> He had a technique for this which he used occasionally in the middle of the night to return to his own room without waking her. Mostly she chucked him out with no ceremony. She preferred to sleep alone and he had learned from experience that the morning glory of Mrs Bhoolaboy's conjugal contentment (a rare bloom) withered rapidly if she did not find herself alone, even if she had not personally dismissed him because incapable

of doing so (pole-axed, he liked to think, by a particularly passionate five-star performance on his part).

The immediate framework of the story is the relationship between the Smalleys and Mrs Bhoolaboy, tenants and landlady respectively, as they struggle to achieve very different aims: the Smalleys to remain in the lodge at Smith's Hotel as legitimate tenants, Mrs Bhoolaboy to evict them in order to profit from the redevelopment of her property in partnership with the owners of the neighbouring Shiraz Hotel. In the course of this tussle, Tusker is driven to a level of apoplexy that proves fatal, his demise forming the opening sentence of the book.

However, the larger picture is of Tusker and Lucy's existence as they move from the relatively sheltered waters of colonial India out into the open seas of an independent country where Tusker's inadequacies are horribly exposed. By 1972, when a sudden collapse suggests his days may be numbered, he has retreated into pathological obstinacy, and Lucy's frustrations find expression as she finally faces up to the prospect of being left alone in India, without the means to return 'home'.

Over the setting of the novel looms the modern five-storey block of the Shiraz Hotel, a metaphorical and literal shadow that has fallen over the Smalleys' lives as their own settle into a steady decline. Scott offers no cosy solution to their problems; and yet you close the book finally not with a sense of gloom but with the satisfaction of having shared with the author 'the comedy of life'. I don't know whether Mussoorie's Carlton Hotel has its own Shiraz Hotel to contend with these days, but I hope the comedy of life is still playing there too.

ANNABEL WALKER is the author of *Aurel Stein: Pioneer of the Silk Road*, a biography of a once famous archaeological explorer.

Blame It on Matron

CHRISTIAN TYLER

Usually, when I discover a second-hand bookshop, I confine my browsing to one or two familiar categories. Military history is not one of them, nor is psychology. So it was by sheer fluke that I recently came upon Norman Dixon's book among tottering piles of volumes. The title, *On the Psychology of Military Incompetence*, jumped out at me. Who could resist it?

On the way home I wondered why I had found the title so appealing, and why I had felt a shiver of *schadenfreude* as I handed over my fiver.

Like all children who grew up in the shadow of the Second World War, I was taught that our side could do no wrong. At school we read comic strips in which square-jawed Spitfire pilots sent Messerschmitts spinning to earth in flames. Black-faced British commandos burst into enemy bunkers where German officers with contorted faces had time only to yell '*Donner und Blitzen!*' before being mown down by tommy-guns. We were thrilled, too, to discover that our gloomy old Classics master had been at the siege of Kut in 1915. He had survived, he told us, by eating rats and reading Homer's *Iliad* – in Greek, of course.

My favourite picture book was *Glorious Battles of English History*. Victories were glorious, but defeats were often more glorious still. In our family – military on both sides, with more than its quota of wounded, dead and decorated heroes – a phrase like 'military

---

Norman F. Dixon, *On the Psychology of Military Incompetence* (1976)
Pimlico · Pb · 448pp · £12.99 · ISBN 0712658890

incompetence' was not just an oxymoron, it was an incendiary device. To suggest that Singapore, Dresden or Hiroshima might have been mistakes was an impertinence bordering on treason. How could I talk, when I hadn't been there? I began to feel ashamed that I had not managed myself to go over the top at Passchendaele, and I worried how I would have acquitted myself. 'Every man thinks meanly of himself for not having been a soldier,' said Samuel Johnson. Too right.

I developed a defensive antipathy to all things military. Brasso and Blanco became my special hates. I took refuge in the belief that most military leaders – apart, of course, from the dashing Alexander of Macedon – were bull-headed and stupid, and that anyone with brains would give the army a wide berth. Then, at my grandmother's house, I was introduced to General Sir Richard O'Connor. He was short and thoughtful, and he talked to me as if I were an equal. Overnight, my prejudices underwent a savage revision.

Norman Dixon's book, bought on impulse, was a revelation. It contained a whole chapter on the fiasco of Kut, more than justifying my old teacher's lugubrious mien. Another analysed, in pages terrible to read, the fall of Singapore. And there were two laudatory mentions of my grandmother's friend General O'Connor, confirming his reputation as one of the great commanders of his time.

Dixon's theme is the psychological battleground over which soldiers (and, *a fortiori*, generals) must fight. Incompetence, Dixon says, is the result of an inability to manage the inner conflict between the dictates of conscience and the need to show real aggression when you are subjected to extreme outside pressure, the 'fog of war'. Prey to their own anxieties, bad commanders become too cautious or not cautious enough. They strike out blindly, or they freeze.

His book begins by describing famous military blunders, from the Crimean War ('the worst managed campaign in British military history') to Arnhem. Dixon was struck by the similarity of the apparently senseless actions – or inactions – of the men in charge. From this 'hairline crack' he developed a hypothesis based on the conviction that something deeper than bad judgement, or bad luck, was at work.

Surrendering Singapore, 1942

Why did a man as charming and intelligent as Major-General Sir Charles Townshend show such wanton disregard for his men's lives? Nearly 40,000 men died as a result of his foray through Mesopotamia (modern Iraq) which ended at the siege of Kut. Why, faced with insurrection in Kabul in 1842, did the courteous Major-General Elphinstone do nothing for so long that his eventual retreat ensured the death by frostbite or at the hands of Afghan tribesmen of almost his entire force of 4,500 and thousands more camp followers? At the fall of Singapore in 1942 nearly 140,000 men were killed or captured and vast amounts of matériel were lost. Why did the commander, the 'brilliant' Lieutenant-General Percival, ignore the pleas of subordinates and superiors to prepare a defence against the approaching Japanese army, insisting that defence would be 'bad for the morale of troops and civilians'?

Dixon knows something of the military mind: he was ten years in the Royal Engineers, where he worked in bomb disposal and was wounded, 'largely due to my own incompetence'. Leaving the army in 1950, he took up psychology and rose to become Professor of Psychology at University College, London. The aim of his book is to scotch the idea that military incompetence is due to stupidity – the 'bloody fool' theory. Bad generals are not stupid, he says. What they lack is imagination, flexibility and independence of mind.

A closer inspection of blundering commanders reveals men of precarious self-esteem, jealous, obstinate, dishonest, vain, subservient and short on moral courage – all symptoms of the 'weak ego'. General Percival, says Dixon, may have been unsure of his masculinity and, like the factory worker who refuses to wear ear plugs, refused to take defensive measures because defence is not 'manly'; it was not the morale of his troops that was imperilled, but Percival's own. These traits are typical of the 'authoritarian' personality. Authoritarians, Dixon explains, are autocrats gone wrong. Although giving every appearance of being in command, they operate out of weakness, not strength. And what makes an authoritarian?

Why, potty training, of course.

At this point, I confess, I thought the author had lost the plot. But I was in too deep to pull back. The product of strict mothers and status-conscious fathers, authoritarians are frigid, frustrated, self-absorbed, superstitious and racist. At prep school the officer classes would be deprived of their (dominating) mothers, and subjected to the ministrations of the headmaster with his cane, and of the matron with her clipboard charting the morning's bowel movement. (Anyone remember?) What better training for the anal retentive! At public school they would be immersed in militarism: the emphasis on sport and muscular Christianity, on amateurism and the hierarchy, on absolute obedience.

Only a small minority of incompetents make it to the top. The big question is how they get there. In the old days, patronage might have accounted for it. Today, a more subtle answer is required, and Dixon provides it.

Authoritarians are naturally attracted to the armed forces. It is the place they feel safest. Drill and ceremonial, obsessive cleaning and polishing, strict authority – 'bull', in short – serve the military purpose of making fighting forces cohesive. But militarism also magnifies the weaknesses of weak egos, and favours the type. What is more, these weak egos are driven to seek promotion – not by a healthy wish to succeed but by a neurotic compulsion to bolster self-esteem. They are like people who climb mountains to cure a fear of heights. And the result is the same: above a certain level they are reduced to frozen immobility.

Outrageously, but intriguingly, Dixon draws on the personalities of Nazi monsters to illustrate his theme. He finds in Townshend of Kut the same kind of vanity as in Hermann Goering. The private obsessions of Field Marshal Lord Haig resembled those of Heinrich Himmler: both had timetable mania and both suffered psychosomatic disorders. Both men presided over mass slaughter, one 'legitimately' on the battlefield, the other criminally in the gas ovens.

You would not guess from all this that Dixon is a witty writer. But he has a nice line in irony, and he writes well. Describing the army's painful conversion from horses to tanks, he notes that Field Marshal Montgomery-Massingberd, chief of the Imperial General Staff, responded to Hitler's rearmament in the 1930s by indenting for a tenfold increase in the budget for motor fuel – and for the same multiple increase in the (much bigger) budget for hay.

Since its publication in 1976 Dixon's book has been quoted by management gurus and got on to the reading lists of bodies such as the Royal Air Force's leadership training centre. But how will his theory stand up in future?

Dixon predicted that military blunders would continue to occur, even though the cost of war – not least the cost of weaponry – would keep going up, and the price of military failure with it. Military thinking might have become more sophisticated, but there are more niches now for incompetents to fill as staffs become larger and battlefield control more remote. War has changed, too. One kind of personality is needed to manage nuclear deterrence, quite another to run military peacekeeping missions among civilians, as Iraq today reminds us. Wars run by committees of politicians and generals are particularly likely to go wrong, according to Dixon. Committees, he says, foster an illusion of invulnerability, under-estimation of the enemy, disregard of contradictory intelligence, and an unquestioned belief in the morality of the group which allows its members to 'overlook the ethical consequences of their decision'. Sounds familiar?

It is possible that Dixon, like Freud, over-elaborated his theory in order to make it fit, and I suspect there is a certain amount of circular reasoning. But, as with Freud, the real meat is in the case studies. For myself, I was pleased to see my youthful distrust of militarism so thoroughly vindicated.

But the further I read, the less smug I felt. By the time I had finished this fascinating book, I was finding my own character defects on every page. I was positively psycho-hypochondriac. Now at least I know that, even if I might not actually have run away, I would most certainly not have made a general. Dixon, disarming to the end, says the same of himself. Hats off to him!

As a writer of non-fiction, CHRISTIAN TYLER has been rude about psychoanalysis for most of his career. Now he is having to eat his words: he is attempting to write a novel.

Southern Crosses

PEGRAM HARRISON

Like Flannery O'Connor, I was born in Georgia. I used to have a thick Southern accent, until my momma hired a British nanny to wallop it out of me; Momma reckons that's why I live in London now. But if I start missing home, I can always dip into O'Connor's fiction from the Deep South of the 1940s and '50s. She never lost her accent, and you can hear it on every page of everything she ever wrote.

Wise Blood brings it out best. It's a novel that might seem stylized and artificial to someone who hasn't spent an afternoon driving a slow car through rural Georgia, listening to the God-bothered radio preachers with their nasal twang. The novel is full of these creatures. Hoover Shoats tells us he 'was on the radio for three years with a program that give real religious experiences to the whole family. Didn't you ever listen to it – called Soulsease, a quarter hour of Mood, Melody, and Mentality. I'm a real preacher, friend.' Blind Asa Hawks, with his sex-crazed daughter Sabbath, hands out tracts saying 'Jesus Loves YOU', while calling out 'If you won't repent, give up a nickel. I can use it as good as you. Wouldn't you rather have me beg than preach?' And chief among these cynical grotesques is a fierce enigma of a man named Hazel Motes.

Hazel arrives in an unnamed, unreal city, fleeing Christ. He's been raised by a country preacher and he can't rid himself of the taint of prophecy, however much he tries. Everything he attempts moves him closer to Jesus, and enrages him further. Even when he was a child,

---

Flannery O'Connor, *Wise Blood* (1949)
Faber · Pb · 176pp · £6.99 · ISBN 0571116124

'there was already a deep wordless conviction in him that the way to avoid Jesus was to avoid sin' – so there really is no escape. Every hat he wears makes him look like a preacher; train travellers and used car salesmen and soda-fountain waitresses all think he's a preacher; a taxi driver tells him, 'It ain't only the hat. It's a look in your face somewheres.' The novel follows Hazel's constant attempts to combat his fate. He finds his way to a brothel: 'Listen, I come for the usual business . . . I ain't no goddam preacher' – to which the lady replies with sleek irony, 'That's okay, son. Momma don't mind if you ain't a preacher.'

O'Connor explores this theme of the Christian *malgré lui* in most of her work. In her second novel, *The Violent Bear It Away* (1955), Francis Marion Tarwater of Powderhead, Tennessee, is like a younger Hazel Motes, anointed to prophesy by his fiery, dying uncle. *Everything that Rises Must Converge* (1956) and the posthumous *Collected Stories* (1971) show precursors and inheritors of these burdened, haunted, intensely comic characters – people fighting to get out from under a yoke. Such freedom, O'Connor observed in a preface to the second edition of *Wise Blood*, 'is a mystery and one which a novel, even a comic novel, can only be asked to deepen'.

Most people in the South know and read O'Connor, even from childhood; she is canonical, a literary icon, a local girl made good. A Roman Catholic in the Protestant Bible Belt, she can be pitched as a religious writer who grapples with obsession and spiritual conflict and the general vertigo of faith within a dismembered modernity. More than this, she's a comic writer with a fiercely hilarious, gothic aesthetic and a completely unfettered savagery.

Much of her fiction also involves hideously ill-behaved children running rings around their elders. My favourites are two little hellions named June Star and John Wesley from a story collection called *A Good Man Is Hard to Find* (1953). They end up dead, but not before sassing their elders over every minute of a long drive in the country: 'Let's go through Georgia fast so we won't have to look at it much . . .

Tennessee is just a hillbilly dumping ground.' Partly because they're jumping around so much, the car rolls over into a ditch: '"We've had an ACCIDENT!" the children screamed in a frenzy of delight. "But nobody's killed," June Star said with disappointment as her grandmother limped out of the car.'

Everybody finally does get killed, in a coldly excessive dénouement, by an escaped convict – a spiritually furious villain named 'The Misfit' who picks off the family one by one. The grandmother is the last to go, after working herself up into the ecstatic belief that The Misfit is her own son – 'one of my babies, one of my own children!' Disturbed by this form of charitable forgiveness, The Misfit kills her brutally and intones a grimly comic backcountry epitaph: 'She would of been a good woman if it had been somebody there to shoot her every minute of her life.'

O'Connor's fictions may start out like fables, or cautionary tales by Belloc, but they end up nearer the spiky moral world of Waugh and Greene and Muriel Spark. Characters in these writers' novels can become ferociously resentful about being redeemed without having had any choice in the matter; about having to put up with moral restrictions on their behaviour and with generally hideous fellow-Catholics; about being so utterly, thoroughly, eternally under the thumb of a higher power, as if they were children. And it is the children and young people and misfits in O'Connor's writing who act with viciousness and wit, because this returns to them a momentary measure of power in a universe that claims arbitrary authority over them. The effort generally destroys both them and those around them, but it brings completeness of a sort.

Among these is Enoch Emory, the 18-year-old moron who gives *Wise Blood* its title. Enoch has 'wise blood like his daddy'. There are no other words for his condition: loose translations like 'instinct', or 'the courage of his convictions' or 'obsessive-compulsive mania' lack the poetry and mystery that give the phrase its power. We see what wise blood does to Enoch, and what it makes him think and do, without ever really knowing what it is. He steals a mummy out of a museum to be a 'new Jesus' and beats up a man to get his gorilla costume – all because his blood tells him to.

I love Enoch for the spirited parade of simile he provokes in O'Connor. Enoch 'looked like a hound-dog with light mange'; his 'heart began to grip him like a little ape clutching at the bars of its cage'; his prattling conversation so vexed Hazel Motes that Motes's face 'looked as if it had a shout closed up in it; it looked like one of those closet doors in a gangster picture where someone is tied to a chair behind it with a towel in his mouth'. This sort of hyperbolic simile is certainly very common in the South ('hotter than Georgia asphalt', 'serious as a heart attack') but in O'Connor's deft comic hands it takes on a spiritual dimension. Enoch is like a sinner or a prophet – and it's hard to tell which in this decayed, sub-rational and thoroughly scrambled version of Christian faith.

The scene with the gorilla suit is a fabulous allegory of misunderstood faith in redemption: Enoch observes a marketing stunt to promote a movie about a gorilla, involving a man in a costume shaking hands with children: 'GONGA! Giant Jungle Monarch and a Great Star! HERE IN PERSON!' He desires the same unconditional respect and even love that he sees the children giving the gorilla. So he steals the costume (deviously and violently) and, having donned this new armour of faith, naturally now repulses everyone he meets.

Hazel Motes flees God by founding his own church, the Church Without Christ. He stands on the hood of his car, 'a high rat-colored Essex', preaching that there is no sin, no blasphemy, no redemption, no belief. From the start it is clear to all but Hazel himself that he protests too much – he who from the age of 12 'saw Jesus move from tree to tree in the back of his mind'. His Church (like his rickety old car) never gets going; various figures block his way either malevolently or with a faint whiff of salvation about them.

When someone pushes Hazel's car off a cliff, destroying his platform and his means of flight, this nonetheless clears the way for him to live his complicated faith rather than rant about it. He mortifies his flesh, and in doing so at last attracts a real convert, someone who had never listened to him preach nor would ever have been moved by mere words. This woman has had a dull life, 'without pain and without pleasure', and now finds both in Hazel. She tells him his self-abnegation is not normal – 'it's something that people have quit doing, like boiling in oil or being a saint or walling up cats' – but nonetheless she is transfigured by it, and begins to perceive the deepening mystery of being.

These people have no apparatus for understanding the shattered world they live in; because of this, repellent though most of them are, they seem to me sympathetic. Motes is a monster, Enoch is pitiful, and I'm no Catholic – but *Wise Blood* is a moving and haunting novel that sounds like home.

PEGRAM HARRISON differs from Flannery O'Connor in other respects beyond living in London, having no southern accent and professing no faith: unlike her, he has never bred peacocks, and has no plans to die at the age of 39. Instead, he teaches at Regent's College and Birkbeck.

Reading the Play's the Thing

CHRISTOPHER RUSH

In 1954, when I was 10, the first twelve-inch, black-and-white television to arrive in St Monans was wheeled into the upstairs living-room of our neighbours across the street, where it caused an immediate sensation. Not even the Coronation the previous year, with all its bonfires and fireworks and beflagged fishing vessels fluttering on the firth, made quite the same impression. The Coronation had been a nine-day build-up and a one-day wonder, disappearing as fast as the bar of chocolate I was given, bearing the new queen's image. But that television altered the very fabric of life.

In fact life died in that first house to usher in the new dispensation. Its owner had a passion for collecting dung, which on a daily basis he dug and raked lovingly into his vegetable patch. He was forever scouring the streets in the wake of the horses that brought round our morning milk in churns, and his was a familiar figure to be seen with sack and shovel, bent over the steaming heaps of newly laid manure. Now the horse dung grew cold on the roads and the green weeds strangled his leeks. The lights went out in his living-room, never to be seen again in my village lifetime.

They were replaced by a cold blue flickering against which the black humps of heads and shoulders gloomed like phantoms. The whole family sat in a stone circle, gorgonized by technology. Soon the circle widened, became a double circle, three tiers, a congregation – the neighbours were pouring in, to a house previously unvisited, arriving on all sorts of pretexts ('Grandad had a good catch this morning – thought you could use these extra haddock') – and staying till the Epilogue and what was now 'God Save Our Queen'. Folk even huddled in knots on the street outside BBC House, as we called it, straining to catch a glimpse of the future, though the upstairs location made it, of course, quite impossible to see a single inch out of the twelve. Football and boxing matches were in full flow, and the deprived stood on the pavement below, intent on those windows, as if it were possible to interpret the firefly flashes of light as goals scored or knock-out punches landed; though in reality the wireless commentaries were far more dramatic than anything the eye could witness.

But the age of the ear and the inner eye was gone for good. The need to see spread madly and a rash of televisions broke out in every window. Soon the streets became like graveyards, the eeriness increased by the phantom flickering that played like lightning in every grove, in every crescent. A forest of masts rocked gently on the roofs, mimicking those in the harbour. 'The light burns blue,' says Brutus, as Caesar's ghost appears in his tent on the eve of Philippi. And blue indeed was the colour of the ghost-town we became.

Once I looked out of our televisionless living-room, still healthy with light, to see an amazing sight. An elderly accountant, whom I'd never seen travelling at anything less dignified than a snail's pace, was propelling himself at startling speed from the bus-stop to his house, just a few yards round the corner. His umbrella preceded him like a rifle, and his scarf and hat were flying as he yomped his way home. England and Scotland were playing at five. I looked at the clock. It was a quarter past. He'd missed the first fifteen minutes. This was serious stuff. And it struck me that an invention which emptied the streets, fossilized families, gave grey hairs wings and allowed me to raid the neighbour's strawberry patch unhindered, simply had to be reckoned with. I began to join in the chorus of childish treble voices begging for a television to be installed 'in our house'. Within a short time my entreaties were answered.

For me it proved a huge let-down – the stilted studio dramas, *Children's Hour*, Andy Pandy, the intermissions, the breakdowns, the white noise. I quickly rediscovered my playgrounds on the bouldered beaches and in the cobbled closes of the village where I'd grown up: a village of a thousand souls whose ten (yes, ten) churches spouted a hell-fire far more fascinating than anything that television could invent. I then proceeded to secondary school in Anstruther, spent four years ignoring the perfectly decent education which my teachers tried to instil in me, and at the end of 1959, having failed all my exams, contemplated my sixteenth year and a career in the Navy.

Which very nearly happened. And I could never have guessed that it would be television that was destined to alter dramatically the course of my life. Up to no good as usual, pinching apples possibly, I fell from a tree and hurt my skull, not seriously, but painfully enough to go reeling home to recover. As I sat there dazed in front of the television, a film started. It was Laurence Olivier's version of *Richard III*. I was 15. And I was transfixed.

More than transfixed. I was transformed. I persuaded my mother to spend 16 precious shillings on the *Oxford Shakespeare* and proceeded to work my passage through the plays, starting with *The Tempest* on p.3 and ending with *Pericles* on p.1072. I read all the poems and sonnets too, and even the glossary. Then I began all over again. I completed this Elizabethan readathon five times in the course of my (repeated) fourth year of secondary schooling, a year of sheer intoxication in which not a day went by but I read a Shakespeare play. At weekends and in the holidays I found I could devour five plays a day. I must have read *Hamlet* alone fifty times at least during that year. After that I threw myself into reading all the great criticism and scholarship, all the standard works, one teacher supplying me with books of his own and with dozens more borrowed from university libraries. Actually my teachers thought (not without enthusiasm) that I'd taken leave of my senses.

And, in a sense, I had. I was beside myself with the sheer joy of literary discovery. I was, in the true meaning of the word, ecstatic. A further two years of secondary schooling, four years of university and three decades of school teaching did much to calm the initial excitement and intellectualize the emotion; but while greater understanding inevitably increased and enhanced enjoyment, there was no recapturing that mad blaze of first love, with all its dizzy raptures.

That is what I want to share with you, the reader: the remembered experience of first literary love. Because, in spite of the fact that it was a film that acted as the trigger, the affair that followed was wholly a matter of reading – solitary, silent, secret, almost illicit – a drama enacted not so much in the closet as in fields and woods, on beaches and haystacks and buses and trains. Anywhere but on a stage or screen. Above all else, it was enacted in the mind.

And I want to ask you a question: how long is it since you actually sat down and *read* a Shakespeare play, for the sheer pleasure of it, as you would read a novel, for example, or a volume of verse? How long is it, come to that, since you read a Shakespeare play at all? Schooldays? Student days? Last time you had to teach it as a text? – all of which involve reasons and feelings that tend to counteract and contradict the pleasure. I have no doubt that if you set out now anew, with pleasure alone in mind, you might be surprised at the kind and degree of it that awaits you, coming over you with the thrill of forgotten delight – *like the sweet sound that breathes upon a bank of violets, stealing and giving odour*, so I am tempted to add.

For this is what it is all about: language, and the use of it by the world's greatest writer. In his *Poetics*, Aristotle outlined the different kinds of pleasure obtainable from drama: Plot, Character, Diction, Thought, Music and Spectacle. Leaving aside music, you may interest yourself primarily in questions that attach to the structure, psychology, language and themes of the play. Alternatively you may leave all that to the scholars and simply go to the theatre, though spectacle does not appear to rank high in the Aristotelian analysis.

You can see why if you read Charles Lamb on Shakespeare. He says in his essay 'On the Tragedies of Shakespeare' (1811) that he went to the theatre ready to be enthralled by the spectacle of humankind battling against the forces of nature – elemental nature and human nature – and what he saw instead was an old actor with a fake white beard tottering about the stage with a stick.

I experienced something similar recently when I went to see Michael Radford's film version of *The Merchant of Venice*, starring Al Pacino as a tired old Shylock and Jeremy Irons as a hopelessly English Antonio, with little of the deep venom you would expect from a hot Hebrew-hater of Renaissance Venice, effete as he may appear in the play. By contrast (apart from reading the play itself) you would do well to return again to Lamb. Have you ever read his essay 'On the Sanity of True Genius', in the *Last Essays of Elia* (1833)? Don't miss it. The relevance to the *Merchant*, I would say, is that Shakespeare may have started out with the idea of writing a play that caricatured a vengeful Jew, but in the end his essential humanity got the better of him and upset the scheme of the drama. Shakespeare was not one to be controlled by the madness of racism, even though his dramatic genius may have lost control of that confused play, and Shylock emerges, in one memorable speech at least, as the mouthpiece for subjugated minorities throughout our world and its shocking history. *If you prick us do we not bleed . . .?*

And have you ever read Coleridge on Shakespeare? During one production he stood up in the stalls and bellowed to the actor playing Shylock to stop grovelling on the ground, to get up on his feet and speak the lines worthy of Shakespeare's creation. Shylock is the tragic hero of the play, for God's sake! (A critical response bettered only by that of the American Civil War soldier who rose from his seat during a production of *Othello* and fired his pistol at the actor playing Iago, just at the climax of the 'fit' scene, where Othello falls to the floor, foaming at the mouth, and Iago gloats, *Work on, my medicine works!* It must have been a convincing performance. The soldier shot Iago dead. The two were buried in the same grave, and their joint epitaph reads: *Here lie the perfect actor and the perfect spectator* – a theatrical critique which might well alarm the acting profession.)

Going back to Coleridge, you won't find inspirational material like his in much of the criticism written since the 1960s. Forget all those clever Oxford men who inhabit the Empire of Dullness. If you want to read criticism which takes you right back to the glowing heart of the drama and rekindles what may be a lost adolescent enthusiasm for the text itself, get yourself a selection of all that Romantic criticism, not forgetting Hazlitt and his dazzling books, *Characters of Shakespeare's Plays* (1817) and *Lectures on the English Poets* (1818). *And with all thy getting, get understanding!* As opposed to obfuscation.

My own first experience of Romantic criticism was taken from that marvellous little volume edited by D. Nichol Smith, *Shakespearean Criticism: A Selection*, first published in 1916 and still easily obtainable. This World's Classics gem was given to me when I was 16 by my History teacher, who gleefully added the extra faggot to the Shakespearean fire that was consuming me. It contains the superb essay by Thomas de Quincey, 'On the Knocking at the Gate in *Macbeth*' (1823), a piece of writing which exemplifies the truth that the best pieces of criticism should be minor works of literature in themselves, best done by writers, not by dons. There is simply nothing like this in contemporary criticism which, with few exceptions (such as John Bayley), takes you away from the text and replaces it with the ivory-towered academic himself, self-admiring on his pedestal.

In the early part of the last century Shakespearean academics were still producing criticism which could be read for its own aesthetic pleasure, besides fulfilling its business of illuminating the text. Aristotle referred to the Plot as 'the soul of tragedy'. Think of a few Shakespearean plots and you may well disagree – till you read Wayne Booth's essay 'Macbeth as Tragic Hero' (1951) or R. S. Crane's *The Language of Criticism and the Structure of Poetry* (1953). If the thematic approach stirs up hateful memories of F. R. Leavis, read L. C. Knights's essays, 'How Many Children Had Lady Macbeth?' (1933), and 'An Approach to *Hamlet*' (1960), still published in various selections. Or read the great J. Dover Wilson, 'What Happens in *Hamlet*' (1935). The title is apt. Wilson sets out to tell you what is really going on in a puzzling play, and he succeeds brilliantly.

All of the above essays feature in a splendid selection of critical extracts put together by Laurence Lerner in 1963, *Shakespeare's Tragedies: An Anthology of Modern Criticism*. Here A. C. Bradley also makes his appearance. First published in 1904, his *Lectures on Shakespearean Tragedy* brought the psychological focus on character to such a point of exhaustive analysis and illumination – so it seemed at the time – that it was felt there was simply nothing left to learn: the bible had been written and the heart of Shakespeare's mystery had been plucked out. One obscure academic even committed suicide. I think, however, that I can safely recommend it. The aura of Edwardian admiration in which Bradley basked is encapsulated in a piece of doggerel which appeared in *The Times* shortly after the book's first publication:

> I dreamt last night that Shakespeare's ghost
> Sat for a Civil Service post.
> The English Papers of the year
> Contained a question on *King Lear*,
> Which Shakespeare answered very badly
> Because he hadn't studied Bradley!

Of course it was all based on the assumption that you could treat plays like novels, even like biographies, and assume that the characters really did have offstage lives, Macbeth and his wife dressing for dinner between foul deeds, an approach on which L. C. Knights famously heaped ridicule in that essay on Lady Macbeth's procreative powers. Nonetheless Bradley's book demonstrates the Shakespearean magic. The master had made you believe, and the disciple (Bradley) helped your unbelief, certainly suspended your disbelief. That suspension had quite a long run. In my own case, if I'd met Hamlet contemplating suicide in St Monans, I'd not have taken him for a ghost. Our rocky coast was Elsinore and *beetled o'er his base into the sea – a sea of troubles*. It was complete captivation.

But in the last analysis it was primarily, as I have said, a matter of language. The plays are great dramatic poems, extended metaphors, and it is in the slightly mad writings of G. Wilson Knight that the poetic worlds of the individual plays are brought brilliantly alive. Read *The Shakespearean Tempest* (1932) or *The Crown of Life* (1947). Above all *The Wheel of Fire* (1932) made me look at *Hamlet* as I'd never seen it before, and though clouded now by some doubt as to its validity, the original impression remains. It is like being guided through Elsinore by William Blake.

It is only when you actually read Shakespeare, however, rather than watch him in action, or study Wilson Knight, that you appreciate the extent to which each play possesses its own peculiar verbal ambience, imparted in its imagery, from the sickening claustrophobia of *Hamlet* ('Denmark's a prison') to the mystical airiness of *The Tempest* ('We are such stuff as dreams are made on/And our little life is rounded with a sleep'). The Elizabethans went to the theatre to hear a play, not to see it, and although it's impossible even for our comparatively cloth ears not to hear familiar lines and phrases being struck like new-minted gold crowns, these verbal atmospheres are at their most pervasive only to the armchair theatre-goer. That solitary experience is what truly allows you to breathe them in and to marvel at the linguistic arrangements, whether it be verbal echoes or leitmotifs, or simply registering the dramatist's endless ability to do different and surprising things with words. The most banal of utterances, by simple repetition, produces a line from *Macbeth* that resonates with all the world-weariness and despair ever experienced by man – *tomorrow and tomorrow and tomorrow* – while the musical pull and counter-pull between the Latinate and the Anglo-Saxon elements in the language, polysyllabic and monosyllabic, are thrown into greater prominence by the act of reading, of actually looking at the words, laid out on a page:

Absent thee from felicity awhile
And in this harsh world draw thy breath in pain
To tell my story.

When Hamlet follows this with 'The rest is silence' (a statement brimming with double meaning) you feel the curtain should come down there. The remaining lines are mere tidying up. And from your fireside chair, *while memory holds a seat in this distracted globe*, you can flash back and direct as you see fit. That moody, introverted, adolescent silence is in fact the way to get the most out of your Shakespeare and his honoured bones. This year Stratford is going to present the Complete Plays. It would be wonderful to attend them all, if practically impossible to achieve. But I have a suggestion to make. Why not read them all first – or instead? If you're busy it might take you a couple of months. If you've nothing else to do it would be a nine-days' wonder. And I'll give you one guess as to who coined that last phrase.

CHRISTOPHER RUSH's memoir of his childhood in St Monans, *Hellfire and Herring*, will be published in January 2007.

Most of the books mentioned here are out of print but may with luck be tracked down in a public library, or via www.abe.com.

Classroom Revolution

PETER BROAD

Let me start with a confession. I too had visited the mobile shop beyond the school gates. I too had crept along the hedgerow into the back of the school, clutching a bulging brown paper bag. I too had stashed away its contents, to be enjoyed in the dorm after lights out.

The mobile shop was, as you would expect, strictly out-of-bounds. Parked at the bottom of the drive of a rural Shropshire prep school, it enticed us with the allure of sweets and the adventure of breaking bounds. The sweets must have been cheap, for our pocket money wasn't more than half-a-crown a week. We stocked up on chewy toffee sticks, pink spearmint, fruit salads – four a penny – and black jacks at the same price. This went on for a fortnight or so, but at some point we must have been spotted sneaking back into the school.

The headmaster stormed into our classroom during prep and made us open our desks and empty our lockers. Now my sweets were zipped up in the ball pocket of a golf bag, which was propped up in the corner of the classroom. As we stood by our desks with the lids up, and as the headmaster examined each desk and emptied each locker, I remember thinking: 'He's sure to look in my golf bag, he hates me playing golf. He thinks I play cricket badly on purpose (and that it's my fault we lost to Abberley last Saturday), and if he does find them, he'll give me more than the others, six at least, for being sneaky . . .' But he didn't look in the golf bag, and I escaped the cane.

My conscience still pricks me when I remember the beatings

Simon Sebag Montefiore, *My Affair with Stalin* (1997)
Phoenix · Pb · 240pp · £6.99 · ISBN 0753801582

received by my fellow adventurers, and now, as a housemaster in a boarding school, my understanding of hypocrisy and irony is sharpened every time I deliver a gentle, but I like to think firm, homily on the importance of being honest. And should any of the boys in my house read this, then I suppose it will have to be a case of 'Do as I say and not as I did.'

For those who have travelled the English boarding-school route, similar prep-school memories are sure to be jogged by reading Simon Sebag Montefiore's *My Affair with Stalin*, a wonderfully entertaining and evocative novel, set in a rural prep school during the 1970s. A daring midnight raid on the tuck cupboard is masterminded by the book's precocious hero, William Conroy. Once he has established control of the cupboard, Conroy is virtually guaranteed his position as leader of the dominant school gang, for crisps, soft drinks and instant snacks play a disproportionately large part in the life of boarding-school pupils.

Inspired by his hero Stalin, Conroy stirs up a revolution in the school which sees the school's *ancien régime*, essentially composed of hearty games players, out-thought, out-manoeuvred and eventually routed by an arty party, made up of clever boys with few if any ball-game skills (aided and abetted by some local lads, bribed on this occasion not with sweets but with cigarettes). That Conroy's regime ends up imposing a tyranny quite as brutal, repressive and intolerant as its predecessor makes comparison with Orwell's *Animal Farm* inevitable.

Not quite an allegory and a bit longer than *Animal Farm* (39 short chapters – ideal for bedtime or, dare I mention it, prep), it is also a shrewd political novel. William Conroy has acquired a thorough knowledge of Stalin's career and methods (in much the same way as contemporaries of mine at prep school seemed to have a comprehensive knowledge of test cricket statistics absorbed from Wisden). Each step of Stalin's rise to power is matched by WC (whose initials can't be accidental) as he enlists the support of the exotic Mendoza to defeat the athletic Dugganoes, capture the Camp (henceforward the

Kremlin) and initiate a reign of terror. The author provides a helpful chronology of the main dates and events of Stalin's career, while such chapter headings as 'The Battle of Stalingrad' point up the parallels between William Conroy and Josef Stalin.

Orwell's classic is not the only point of comparison. Those who have relished Evelyn Waugh's *Decline and Fall* will be amused by the gallery of prep-school pupils, teachers and parents: the teacher whose surname is Allcock, thus giving the boys an opportunity to chorus '. . . and no balls!'; the headmaster, whose electric hair, archaic slang, good humour and lack of worldliness endeared him to me almost as much as the unfortunate teacher whose bald head seems fated to attract the attention of every passing pigeon; and the pupil Mendoza, rich, foreign and frighteningly grown-up, who is brought to school in a chauffeur-driven limousine. Lessons (about which teachers care a great deal) rarely feature, while free time, leisure and after lights out (about which boys care equally passionately) are especially vivid.

In Uncle Joe's footsteps. By David Eccles

The author takes on a third heavyweight contender in William Golding's *Lord of the Flies*. Few of us can read about an English prep school without being reminded of those stranded boys on their tropical island. The violence in *My Affair with Stalin*, however, is tinged with a healthy black humour: during one of Conroy's purges we learn that 'One glimpse of the Bunsen flames was usually enough. But if not, they stoned them in the Fives Courts, dipped their faces in the Chapel font or hung them by their feet off the squash court balcony. In fact those butterfingers dropped Minto. But he survived.' No

Health and Safety officers around in those days.

The author's feel for schoolboy slang is pitch perfect: likewise his depiction of the young teacher Miss Snow's wardrobe, a delicious catalogue of half-forgotten fashions. And Conroy's progress, between the ages of 11 and 13, from victim to bully, from wimp to Alpha Male, is charted with wry detachment by an author for whom the sensations of schoolboy life are still vivid, perhaps even raw.

Quoting from the book is almost irresistible. I love the bathos of Conroy's order to his second-in-command Petty: 'You can arrest him after Scottish Dancing on Friday.' And who could resist the description of the 'brave commissars of the NKVD wearing pyjamas and dressing gowns' or the revelation that the 'bullets were choc-ices stolen from the kitchen'.

William Conroy's affair with Stalin concludes as he begins an affair of a different kind and is introduced to the pleasures of the flesh by the half-Filipina Catalina who works in the school's kitchen. Appropriately the description of their first encounter involves food: 'She put her hand on my shoulder and, once again, she handed me a cake. I swallowed all its chocolate and its pastry before I looked up at her . . . I could have sworn she smelled of warm loaves, maybe the sponge of her cakes.' William is not just precocious intellectually.

And for those who wonder what happens to such precocious young prep-school boys, Simon Sebag Montefiore has gone on to write a scholarly book entitled *Stalin and the Court of the Tsar*.

PETER BROAD is a housemaster at Eton, where he has taught English and Drama for nearly twenty years.

The Maclean Effect

PAUL ROUTLEDGE

I defy anyone to read Fitzroy Maclean's *Eastern Approaches* and not want to go to mysterious Central Asia. From the moment I read those seductive first paragraphs as a student, I was drawn to the murky world of Bokhara, Samarkand and Tashkent that Maclean observed at close quarters in the 1930s when working as a diplomat in our Moscow embassy. It was to be ten years before I travelled to the Soviet Republic of Uzbekistan in the 'year of stagnation' – 1975 – and another three decades before I saw the country without the dubious assistance of a Soviet minder.

But still those opening sentences hold me in thrall. 'Slowly gathering speed, the long train pulled out of the Gare du Nord . . . I was on my way to Moscow, and from Moscow, I was going, if it was humanly possible, to the Caucasus and Central Asia,' wrote Maclean. As he watched the drab, sodden countryside rush past the carriage window, in his mind's eye he saw the green oases, the sunlit domes and minarets of Turkistan. 'Suddenly, as I sat there in the half light, I felt immensely excited.' If there is a more romantic opening to a book, not just a travel book but any book, then I don't know of it.

Maclean's ostensible purpose was a good deal more prosaic. He was leaving a very agreeable posting in Paris to take up an appointment in the embassy in Moscow as military attaché. Friends warned him that the Soviet capital in the 1930s was a dead end, a tedious round of parties in overheated chancelleries where he would meet the

---

Fitzroy Maclean, *Eastern Approaches* (1949)
Penguin · Pb · 576pp · £12.99 · ISBN 0140132716

same people, none of them Russian. At the back of his mind, however, lurked the golden road to Samarkand and 'the lust of knowing what should not be known', in James Elroy Flecker's unforgettable phrase. In the previous century, few Britons had visited this fabled region, and even fewer had returned to tell the tale. Turkistan, a vast area fought over by the warring khanates, had fallen belatedly and reluctantly to the Red Army in 1922. Since then, its crumbling cities, crowded with some of Islam's finest cultural sites, had been off limits to Westerners. The people of Central Asia, their customs and their life under the Soviets were a closed book. Maclean, a young Highland Scot of some impetuosity, but possessed of diplomatic immunity and kitted out with a wry sense of humour, was ideally placed to make 'the golden journey'. That he had an easy, natural style of writing, and had done his historical homework, was a bonus that keeps *Eastern Approaches* in print more than half a century later.

After some furtive exploration of what was then Tiflis (now Tbilisi) and the oil centre of Baku, scene of the alleged massacre of twenty-six commissars by the British in 1918, Maclean felt confident enough to tackle the Asian heart of the USSR. He travelled by rail, to Alma Ata, 'Father of the Apples', capital of remote, empty Kazakhstan, but found, as all travellers do, that there is little to see there except the luminous prospect of the Tien Shan mountains bordering China. He journeyed on to Samarkand via Tashkent, enduring the incompetent attentions of the NKVD, hilariously described. In the city of his dreams, home of Tamerlane's glorious, blue-domed mausoleum, the young diplomat was fascinated by the natives. A young Uzbek woman 'reminded me of a face on a Chinese scroll . . . her features were finely formed and the delicate oval of her face showed a trace of some other ancestry, Persian perhaps, or Circassian'.

Yet he clearly spent only one day in the city of James Elroy Flecker's imagination, drawing literary sustenance from its magnificent minarets. The excursion whetted his appetite for the ultimate destinations: Bokhara and Chinese Turkistan. Stalin's show-trials interrupted his travel plans, and they make chilling reading. By this time he was a 'largely spurious' expert on Central Asia, on the strength of a report written for the Foreign Office after his expedition.

After a failed bid to reach Urumchi, Maclean finally arrived in Bokhara the Noble in the autumn of 1938. From the nearest railhead at Kagan, and after some adventures with the local police, he walked through the night until, topping a slight rise, he looked down on its broad white walls and watchtowers. He followed a string of dromedaries into the city of the emirs, 'very unlike the Soviet Union' but with a red flag fluttering atop the spectacular and infamous Tower of Death from which the Emir casually dispatched his subjects. Maclean waxes lyrical about the blue-tiled mosques and madrasahs, the *chai-khanas*, the busy bazaar and the delights of idling under apricot trees in the clear, warm sunlight of Central Asia. He also relates some adventures of previous British visitors to the city, including the nineteenth-century eccentric, the Reverend Joseph Woolf, who escaped being thrown headlong from the tower by presenting himself to the Emir garbed in full canonicals – clergyman's gown, doctor's hood and shovel hat, a Bible under his arm. His comical appearance, and his readiness to prostrate himself while crying thirty times '*Allah Akbar!*', so amused the despot that he let him go.

Maclean made his way back to Moscow circuitously via Kabul, Peshawar, Baghdad, Tabriz and Yerevan, and there his Asian odyssey ends. The rest of *Eastern Approaches* covers his time with the SAS in the Western Desert, and his hair-raising adventures with Tito's partisans in Yugoslavia, an experience that made him a lifelong friend of both leader and country. These periods make up two-thirds of the book, but they are something of an anti-climax after the magic of Central Asia.

However, the Maclean effect does not end there. It sends you further, deep into the luxuriant thickets of 'Britons in Asia' literature. To begin with, there are Maclean's own later expeditions, which produced *A Person from England* (1958) and *Back to Bokhara* (1959), not

'Very unlike the Soviet Union' but with a red flag fluttering atop the spectacular and infamous Tower of Death. By James Nunn

to mention Frank McLynn's biography of the man, published in 1992. Then there is Colonel F. M. Bailey's *Mission to Tashkent* (1946), James Lunt's *Bokhara Burnes* (1969), and Philip Glazebrook's *Journey to Khiva* (1992). Further back, Arminius Vambery's celebrated *Travels in Central Asia* of 1864 has been republished by the Cambridge Scholars' Press, while a 1983 edition of Fred Burnaby's *A Ride to Khiva* (1877) has a preface by Eric Newby, who was entranced by a book 'so idiosyncratic, so endearing and so funny'– no mean praise from a writer who is all those things himself.

Branch lines radiate everywhere from these beginnings, especially to anything written by Peter Hopkirk. My own 'Maclean library' starts in Belgrade and finishes in Beijing. It takes up practically a whole bedroom wall, and threatens to invade the landing. Hunting down the more exotic titles is a journey in itself, particularly since the arrival of the Internet. How Fitzroy would have despised this ersatz adventurism!

Not until 1975 could I follow in the great man's footsteps. As labour correspondent on *The Times*, I was offered a trip to the USSR, and agreed to go on condition that Central Asia was on the itinerary. In company with Mick Costello of the *Morning Star*, and a minder from the Soviet agency Novosti in Moscow, we got as far as Tashkent, Samarkand and Alma Ata. It was mid-February, and bitterly cold. After the obligatory textile factory and trade-union visits, we squeezed in a day's cultural tourism in Samarkand, which emphatically did not disappoint. Not a great deal, I imagined, had changed since Maclean's foray half a century earlier. We bounced around the Shah-I Zindar complex of mausoleums and mosques, and the blue-ribbed Gur Emir mausoleum, burial place of Timur, in a clapped-out Lada, and drank in a *chai-khana* with bemused Uzbeks who sat cross-legged on the floor. I noticed they were drinking a clear white liquid from delicate china bowls. What might that be? '*Bielo chai*,' they smirked into their moustaches. White tea – vodka! On that expedition, alas, Bokhara was '*niet*'.

Almost three decades more elapsed before I could return, ten years after the end of Soviet Communism but once again in the company of the fluent Russian-speaking Costello. It was now possible to fly direct from London to Tashkent, overnight, in a brand-new Boeing jet, with a driver waiting at the airport to whisk us to a private hotel. Everything certainly had changed in that interval. We saw the splendours of Bokhara, and the bug-pit where in 1842 the British officers Stoddart and Connolly were incarcerated before being executed by the Emir. Through the Kyzyl Kum desert, we penetrated further than Maclean to the even more ancient city of Khiva.

Khiva is now a Unesco world heritage site, infested with carpet-

and souvenir-sellers, virtually a ghost city where the mosques are for tourists, not worshippers. We were there during one of the frequent anti-religious clampdowns ordered by President Ismail Karimov, subsequently to earn the soubriquet of the Butcher of Andijan. The atrocity of May 2005, when at least 500 protesting Uzbeks were mown down by troops in the Ferghana valley bordering Kirghizstan, is a reminder that Central Asia can still be a violent, unpredictable place in spite of all its architectural treasures. The cruel Emir of Bohkara – who fled as late as 1920, 'dropping', as Maclean writes, 'favourite dancing boy after favourite dancing boy in his flight in the hope of thus retarding the advance of the Red Army, who, however, were not to be deterred by such stratagems' – may have gone, but his ways have not.

Still, Maclean is right. Sweet it is to sit under a shady almond tree, by a water-tank, sipping vodka and eating shashlik, with the brilliant blue tiles of a nearby ancient mosque glittering in the sunshine. In that sense, at least, the anticipation roused by Fitzroy Maclean's opening paragraph is not disappointed. And there is always the literature when you get home.

PAUL ROUTLEDGE is a columnist on the *Daily Mirror*, and author of seven books of political biography, including *Public Servant, Secret Agent: The Elusive Life and Violent Death of Airey Neave*.

Artist of Earth and Sky

SIMON BRETT

Despite the aspirations Gwen Raverat expressed in her classic childhood memoir *Period Piece* ('O happy Mrs Bewick!' she declares at one point) and all the drawings in the book, many of its enchanted readers have discovered with apparent surprise that its author was an artist of some importance. Yet this may not be so remarkable; little had been written about her later life until Frances Spalding's full biography in 2001, though Gwen and her husband Jacques did feature in Paul Delaney's *The Neo-Pagans* (1987) as central members of the Cambridge circle surrounding Rupert Brooke. My own journey was in the opposite direction from most people's. I knew Gwen Raverat as an artist long before I discovered *Period Piece.*

She seems to me to be perhaps the only artist in my own medium of wood engraving to whom the adjective 'great' could be applied. Obviously, if greatness consists in producing *grandes machines*, as those vast French exhibition pieces like *The Raft of the Medusa* are called, she is out of the running, for few of her works measure more than four or five square inches. But if greatness may consist in distilling and communicating with rare intensity and consistency the individual vision which most artists only attempt to define, then she might be in there with Rembrandt (whose etchings she kept beneath her pillow as a child) and Samuel Palmer.

Gwen Darwin took up wood engraving before and quite independently of the schools which promoted it in the 1920s; she taught herself to engrave in 1909 while she was at the Slade School of Art, in London. In 1911, she married Jacques Raverat, the English-educated and Anglophile son of a French industrialist. He had

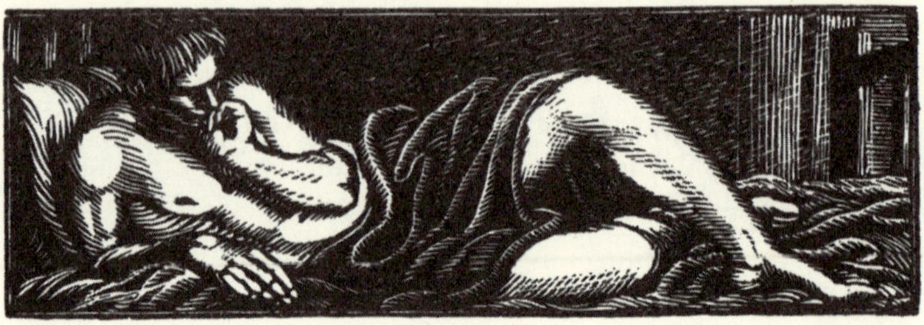

studied mathematics at Cambridge, where they met, but turned to the crafts as a printer, and then to art as a painter, on his doctors' advice. I suppose they thought that, for an invalid, it was less intellectually taxing. Needing to make a life, though with his private income not a living exactly, they lived and worked as artists in various places; and in 1920 moved to the south of France for the sake of his seriously worsening health. He died there of multiple sclerosis in 1925.

Gwen returned to Cambridge and brought up her daughters there. She wrote perceptive art criticism for *Time and Tide* and, largely avoiding the darker themes in the younger work she did with Jacques, focused her engraving on landscape and on illustrating children's books. The most personal of these, *The Runaway*, has been reissued by Persephone. *Period Piece* was not written until she was 64, after a stroke had stopped her engraving – she continued to paint sturdily from her wheelchair.

Gwen Raverat could be seen as the linchpin of many of the interlinked literary and artistic movements which have fuelled British biography for the past thirty years. John Maynard Keynes was her brother-in-law. Her father and Virginia Woolf's father Leslie Stephen were friends. Virginia visited Gwen's home when seeing her brother at Cambridge, and when Gwen went to the Slade she visited Virginia in London. She was the first secretary of Virginia's Friday Club, in at the start of 'Bloomsbury', just as she had been at the heart of Rupert Brooke's Cambridge set.

Virginia Woolf called her a 'monolith', a well-made phrase she liked to return to, as writers will. Certainly, Gwen saw herself as less intellectually clever than the Bloomsburies; certainly, she had a strength that enabled her to nurse Jacques and still (with the domestic help her background provided) to paint for ten hours a day while doing so. But 'monolith' simply does not recognize her sensibility. And both as a person and as an artist, she remains relatively unknown today. The 'little grain of me' she wrote of in *Period Piece* remains hidden – even perhaps from her own biographer. To find it, you have to look at her work.

A definitive selection of her engravings was made by Reynolds Stone and published shortly after her death in 1957. It is long out of print. In 1989, when Faber declared no interest in reprinting it, it was reissued by Silent Books of Cambridge with several pages of additional engravings and a thirty-years-on postscript. That too is out of print. But Joanna Selborne and Lindsey Newman's substantial *Gwen Raverat, Wood Engraver*, published in 1996, is now available in a British Library edition. Two popular selections, *Wood Engravings of Cambridge* and *Gwen Raverat in France*, are published by Broughton House Books, based at the Broughton House Gallery in Cambridge, which holds the Raverat archive. Returning to biographies, Frances Spalding's is now in paperback; and Raverat's grandson, William Pryor, has published a well-illustrated volume of the letters between his grandparents and Virginia Woolf.

In this joyous yet thoughtful exchange, chiefly between Virginia

and Jacques, their remarks about Gwen as though she isn't there form the running joke of the correspondence. Gwen was, in fact, very much there, taking Jacques's dictation from his sickbed but herself remaining almost silent. Two long letters from her, written after his death, begin to balance *Period Piece*, showing her in her maturity, in her own words. The limits of words, the immediacy of painting and Virginia's desire to get that quality into her writing are some of the things Virginia and Jacques discussed.

Jacques's death was a defining event for Gwen. 'There are some things in life', she wrote to Virginia, 'that some of us know about but that it is indecent to write about – some kinds of pain, I think . . . Like the Goya etchings . . . Nobody takes any notice of them or of what they mean because they daren't I suppose.'

Though she retired to emotionally safer ground in the second half of her life, something of the same intensity of feeling permeates a great deal of her work, making it indeed almost 'indecent' to look at. When love – in her case mostly love of place – is very strongly expressed one turns one's eyes away from it, as from pain, in a kind of self-protection. Yet Gwen Raverat is so very far from being naïve that one cannot dismiss her intensity as gush. Maybe this is partly why she remains unseen.

Even Virginia, whose goodness shines from her letters, never quite 'saw' Gwen as an artist, though she valued her deeply as a friend. She could be both cutting about the soulless, dumpy Darwins (Gwen

looked not unlike the French peasant women she engraved) and yet overcome with admiration for the granite of which, she came to see, Gwen was made. For her, she says, Gwen and Jacques had represented what love is.

Yet the work which I think defines Gwen's stature and which all her other work rises towards and falls away from, was made in this second part of her life. The current selections of her work present her as an artist of views and rural life. That is true (and some of her Cambridge townscapes are major works) but it is not the whole truth. One work mainly, the Ashendene Press edition of *Daphnis and Chloe*, shows her in quite another light.

Ashendene was the private press of St John Hornby, owner of W. H. Smith, the man who hired Eric Gill to paint the lettering on his shop fronts. The book was actually *Daphnis et Chloé*, a translation into Renaissance French of the Latin pastoral by Longus, just the sort of rather recherché thing private presses printed then, and sometimes still do. For one of the major 'press' books of the twentieth century, it is small, and surprisingly archaic in its design. The engravings sometimes seem squeezed in alongside the type, where today we might prefer an airier page. But it is what they are that matters. They show a world embraced by light. The dark, symbolist, ballad-inspired engravings of Gwen's student years had given way, in the early years of her relationship with Jacques, to a formalized, black-line style. This starkness had been broken open in its turn by the effects of French light, as their paintings also show.

The forms in *Daphnis et Chloé* are lapped in light, moulded and softened by it. Few of these miraculous images appear in any of the current selections, except for the Selborne & Newman study, but even that, its fine print first edition based on the availability of original blocks, does not present any of the full-page ones. *Daphnis* represents the opposite pole of wood-engraved illustration to, for example, Eric Gill's *The Four Gospels*, another of the great books of the century. Gill's engravings are made of firm black outlines; they partake of the character of type. Raverat's are little worlds of feeling. She rings in the modest medium of wood engraving a Titianesque note, evoking the luxuriance of the bacchanal and, at times, the colder world of the Venetian's later work.

It has been suggested that Eric Gill influenced Gwen, but it is almost certainly the other way round. In 1913 she and Gill and Jacques and Stanley Spencer planned a Gospel book together, foreshadowing *The Four Gospels* which in fact appeared eighteen years later, in 1931. Gill had hardly begun as an engraver in 1913 but Gwen was well established in the art, as he was the first to acknowledge. He offered himself as a sort of kitchen maid to the project, doing the tidying up and the lettering, though it was his insistence on using a text approved by the Catholic Church that eventually caused the project to founder. The images were to be designed by Jacques and engraved by Gwen. The designs owe much to the medieval sculpture of Vézelay, near Jacques's home in Pontigny, as well as to the characteristic, hard-edged clarity which is seen in all his work. Here too, Gwen was in at the beginning of things and at the heart of them in ways which history has not fully recognized.

Though much of Gwen Raverat's work was bespoke illustration, she was not just an artist who put her talent at the service of whatever story she chose or was asked to illustrate. Her images are anchored in a larger sense of how the world is, a vision of how space and form relate and how human life is lived: something more than just a style or an accent, what in a writer would be a 'voice'. This peaks and becomes recognizable in *Daphnis et Chloé.* The new books of the letters and of the French engravings reproduce several of her drawings; how good, how classic, how sensitive and strong they are. The student of her work begins to recognize themes – moments or subjects she chose for personal yet universal reasons. The pupil of Rembrandt here, rather than of the anecdotal Bewick, she evokes an essence of life, in the body, upon the earth, with a simplicity that is the hardest thing to achieve. As an artist of earth and sky she stands with Millet.

Period Piece is a delightful and enduring book; it can lead one fairly directly to the domestic and rural side of Gwen Raverat's work as an artist and it preserves for all time her humour and her personal charm; but it was an afterthought, peripheral to what she was really about, a bubble on the deeper stream of another sort of purely visual achievement, which is very much worth investigating.

SIMON BRETT edited the 1989 edition of *The Wood Engravings of Gwen Raverat.*

The following books featuring Gwen Raverat's work are still in print:
Joanna Selborne & Lindsay Newman, *Gwen Raverat, Wood Engraver* (1996) · British Library · Hb · 152pp · £35 · ISBN 0712347925; Rosemary Davidson (ed.), *Gwen Raverat: Wood Engravings of Cambridge and Surroundings* (2003) · Broughton House · Hb/Pb · 96pp · £15.95/£11.95 · ISBNs 0954391705 and 0954391713; Rosemary Davidson (ed.), *Gwen Raverat in France* (2004) · Broughton House · Hb/Pb · 80pp · £16.95/£12.95 · ISBNs 0954391721 and 095439173X; William Pryor (ed.), *Virginia Woolf and the Raverats* (2003) · Clear Books · Hb · 206pp · £16.99 · ISBN 1904555020; Frances Spalding, *Gwen Raverat: Friends, Family, Affections* (2001) · Pimlico · Pb · 438pp · £18 · ISBN 1844134245; Elizabeth Anna Hart, *The Runaway* (1872), with wood engravings by Gwen Raverat · Persephone · Pb · 232pp · £12 · ISBN 1903155266.

All the engravings in this article are from *Daphnis et Chloé.* A review by HAZEL WOOD of *Period Piece* appeared in Issue 8 of *Slightly Foxed.*

A Curse Against Book Stealers

Illustrated by DAVID ECCLES

Recently, we came across an intriguing notice pinned up on a board in the college library at Peterhouse, Cambridge, and we couldn't resist reproducing it here. 'A Curse Against Book Stealers' allegedly comes from the Monastery of San Pedro in Barcelona, but whatever its provenance we thought it might strike a chord.

There is nothing more maddening than lending a book to a friend who never returns it. Years later, dimly remembering that wonderful treatise on the delights of eating oysters, and wanting to reread it, you go to look for it. It should be on the second-to-top shelf, in between Richard Mabey's *Food for Free* (bought when you were a penniless student) and John Seymour's *Self-Sufficiency* (acquired a little later on, when the Good Life seemed, well, a good idea). But it isn't. And of course you can no longer remember who the friend was, though whether he or she would still be a friend if you did is now a moot point. Never mind. The Curse is to hand.

FOR HIM that stealeth a Book from this Library, let it change into a Serpent in his hand and rend him. Let him be struck with Palsy, and all his members blasted. Let him languish in Pain crying aloud for mercy, and let there be no Surcease to his Agony till he sink to Dissolution. Let Bookworms gnaw his Entrails in token of the Worm that dieth not, and when at last he goeth to his final Punishment let the flames of Hell consume him forever and aye.

Big Windies

JOHN HARRISON

The lady at the Aerolineas Isla Robinson Crusoe desk greeted me by name, though we'd never met. Her passenger list comprised three words: Señor John Harrison. The six-seater Cessna was piloted by a handsome 30-year-old trying to look like an extra for *Top Gun*, and doing rather well. We left the heat of Chile's vineyards behind us, arrowing over the Pacific, aiming at a myth. Conditions were calm, despite the receptionist's warning: 'There is a lot more weather on the island than here: big windies.'

The Juan Fernández Islands, 400 miles offshore, were discovered in 1572 by a Spanish priest and navigator who modestly named them after himself. Failing to make a go of a settlement, he left only goats as a memorial. The main island became a mid-oceanic convalescent stop, providing wood, fresh water, fruit, turnips planted by mariners, and the tasty descendants of Father Juan's goats. It's not so welcoming for aircraft; when I saw the landing strip, I had big windies myself. We shot down a dirt runway that began at the cliff edge, ran across a narrow neck of land, and squealed into a U-turn yards from the opposing cliff top. Top Gun grinned. 'Madness!'

I first met *Robinson Crusoe* when I was 8, in a hardback children's edition with a red cloth cover whose edges I stroked as I read, curled up in an armchair. It had footnotes (so grown up) to explain delicious

---

Daniel Defoe, *Robinson Crusoe* (1719)

Penguin · Pb · 288pp · £4.99 · ISBN 0141439823
A beautifully produced hardback edition is also available in the Everyman's Library Children's Classics series · Hb · 464pp · £10.99 · ISBN 1857159187

antique words like pannikin, pipkin and calenture (a tropical delirium in which the sailor believes the sea to be green fields, and tries to leap into it). Before starting to read, I looked at the frontispiece, showing a man in a goatskin suit with matching umbrella, then at each illustration in turn, imagining how the plot would stitch them together, writing my own story. When I finished the book, my mother helped me place the kitchen table upside-down on the lawn. Each heavy round leg was held in place by a single wing-nut. I removed two and propped them over the side: my cannons. A Union Jack, tied to a third, marked the stern. Brothers and friends were press-ganged as crew, though they soon died in a shipwreck and were told to wait on one side until required for the cannibal feast.

Robinson Crusoe is a simple stereotype; he is you and me forced back on to our own resources. He was inspired by the true adventures of the Scottish sailor Alexander Selkirk, an able but short-fused officer on the privateer *Cinque Ports*, who was left in the Juan Fernández Islands on Más a Tierra, now renamed Isla Robinson Crusoe. Selkirk had demanded to be marooned after he had pronounced the *Cinque Ports* unseaworthy, and Captain Thomas Stradling, just 21, had refused to tarry for repairs. Selkirk's chest was fetched, and a few other items, including a musket, powder and shot. Only as the ship's boat began to pull away did Selkirk realize the enormity of what he was doing and beg them to return. Stradling said, 'Stay where you are, and may you starve.' Thankfully for Defoe and us, he didn't.

At Cumberland Bay, the only settlement on Isla Robinson Crusoe, I was met by a porter with a wheelbarrow. 'Come this way, Señor Harrison, I'm Robinson Green.' After finding a room in a modest guesthouse, it took me over an hour to climb 1,700 feet, through lush vegetation jewelled with flowers and hummingbirds, to the summit which provided Selkirk's view over the anchorage. The whole island is a volcano lying on one of the most dangerous fault lines in the world. It is a place which makes you feel the land is only borrowed from the sea. In one earthquake, the sea receded until it was scarcely visible, before returning to crash a hundred feet up the hillside, destroying everything in its path.

But however carefully you have read the book, the island will not seem familiar. Defoe moved the whole adventure 3,000 miles across the South American land mass to an imaginary island near Trinidad. Perhaps details of the Caribbean were easier to come by, for Defoe, a pamphleteer and reporter, loved detail. And though *Crusoe* is inspired by Selkirk, it is not Selkirk's story. There is evidence that Selkirk later gave his papers to Daniel Defoe, but none that they ever met.

Defoe's own life was as interesting as Selkirk's; he had been a spy, had suffered the pillory, had been condemned for treason then reprieved, had gone bankrupt, and, in a fury of creativity, wrote four novels in two years, including *Crusoe*. The haste shows in the writing: Crusoe strips to swim out to a ship wrecked on the reef but he is mysteriously able to stuff salvaged goods into his trouser pockets. His ink runs out, but he continues to write. Even so, the novel makes us imagine how we would cope in similar circumstances.

In fact, Crusoe is unrealistically rational, doing the things a writer safe in a study thinks he'd do: salvage tools and provisions from the ship. In reality, new castaways are numb with shock: they lie helpless, or wander without purpose, or immerse themselves in trivial tasks. Selkirk, although set ashore in good health, lay all night in a stupor, terrified by strange roars that daylight revealed to be fur seals. Only when parched with thirst did he take command of himself and get organized.

He'd chosen a good spot. I have sailed all along the west coast of South America, and I can think of nowhere safer or more congenial to live off the land than Juan Fernández: the climate is kind and food abounds. At different times, others were also marooned here; all lived comfortably. Selkirk himself was fitter than the scurvy-ridden sailors who tottered ashore to rescue him four years and four months later.

The book is also a moral allegory. Before Crusoe ran away to sea, his father gave him very English advice about ambition: have some, but not too much; the middle class enjoys the virtues of the other two classes and the vices of neither. But Crusoe is 'born to be my own destroyer'. After a good start in trade, he leaves his sugar plantation in Brazil to undertake a slaving voyage. Deserting the cultivation of the land for a quick doubloon, he is punished by shipwreck. He now slaves himself, to plant corn and bake bread. He bodges together an oven, and eventually produces a loaf.

As a child, I asked 'Why bother, when there was so much else to eat?' But Defoe knew his readers could not consider Crusoe happy until he had bread and butter, earned by the sweat of his brow. In an age of expansion and change, Defoe reminded the English of where they sprang from. For the mass of ordinary people, life was a little more comfortable than that on a desert island, but prosperity was fickle, as they and Defoe knew first-hand. Crusoe showed them that whatever fate had in store, an industrious Protestant Englishman could overcome it.

Defoe is very good on anxiety. I've often travelled rough in South America and fretted over food supplies, though, unlike him, I've seldom had to worry about becoming someone else's dinner. But, like Crusoe, I know that it is not fear of wild animals that keeps you awake at night, it's fear of people. Defoe presents Crusoe with the famous single footprint in the sand, then shows him no more for two years: that is very refined torture. There's soon more to worry about, when his corn is stolen: the thieving crows he shoots are exhibited in chains, like criminals. You can imagine him muttering 'Hangin's too good for 'em.' Pilgrim Crusoe gradually rediscovers God and the unique satisfaction of being an English yeoman farmer. However, solitary reflection does not make him a radical; when he finally gains his famous companion, a local Indian (not the Negro of my old edition), Man Friday is taken on as a servant, not a partner. Crusoe also renames him, that most potent form of possession.

How did Selkirk survive? He was picked up by a Bristol privateer, and his share in the prize money made him a wealthy man. He never blamed himself for abandoning the *Cinque Ports*; it broke up in a storm with the loss of nearly all hands. Returning to Fife, he briefly became a celebrity before shunning society. Pining for his lost kingdom, he dug a cave behind his parents' home and moved in. He later returned to sea, dying in a fever epidemic off Africa. Crusoe was equally restless, living on through two pale sequels.

Doctor Johnson said that *Don Quixote*, *Pilgrim's Progress* and *Robinson Crusoe* were the only three books anyone ever wished were longer. The list hasn't grown much since then. *Robinson Crusoe* is still an escape for me. When it all seems too much, I don't dig a cave, I have a calenture and leap overboard into its perennially green pages. I picture Isla Robinson Crusoe and walk, in memory, the beach where locals have recreated a shelter and propped two salvaged cannons on its ramparts. They look rather like my old table legs.

As JOHN HARRISON posted the manuscript for his travel book, *Where the Earth Ends*, about South America and its islands, he realized every influential text behind it had been read before he was 12 years old, including *Robinson Crusoe*.

Putting the Story into History

JOHN DE FALBE

The year 1905 was not the zenith of the British Empire in territorial terms (surprisingly perhaps, that was 1947, before Indian independence), but imperial confidence was about as high then as it would ever be. No baleful auguries of the Western Front had yet been observed, no rumours of equal political rights for native peoples had reached suburban English parlours. The future would be a triumphant continuation of British supremacy, built on hard-won principles of good governance and justice. There can be few more solid expressions of that faith than the publication, in that year, of the children's history book *Our Island Story* by H. E. Marshall. It is a stirring compendium of tales, beginning with Neptune raising himself from the waves and giving 'his sceptre to the islands called Britannia, for we know: "Britannia rules the waves."'

It proceeds via Romans, Vikings, Normans, Plantagenets, Tudors, Stuarts and Hanoverians to the 'great and glorious reign' of Queen Victoria. But it is not an uncritical chronicle of Kings and Queens. Many of them are roundly condemned as bad, and the narrative is alive with anecdotes of lesser heroes and heroines: Judge Gascoigne, for example, who sent Prince Hal to prison for contempt of court, and Jenny Geddes, who threw a stool at the Dean of St Giles

---

H. E. Marshall, *Our Island Story* (1905)
Galore Park & Civitas · Hb · 512pp · £19.99 · ISBN 1902984749
E. H. Gombrich, *A Little History of the World* (1936)
with illustrations by Clifford Harper
Yale University Press · Hb · 304pp · £14.99 · ISBN 0300108834

in Edinburgh for reading from the new Prayer Book ordered by Charles I. And as early as Edward the Confessor, when he promised the crown of England to his cousin William of Normandy, we read that he 'had no right to do this . . . The kings of England had really no power to act in great matters without calling together a council of the nobles and wise men. The English had always been a free people, who had a share of governing themselves. Their kings had been kings, not tyrants.' However much one might wish to contend the truth of this statement applied to eleventh-century England, it is interesting that it was felt to be a notion suitable for a nursery in 1905.

Many readers will remember, as I do, reading *Our Island Story* when they were children, with its stirring tales of Hengist and Horsa, William the Conqueror, the Siege of Calais, Cromwell and so on. They may also remember the wonderfully dreadful sub-Pre-Raphaelite pictures: Boadicea (looking rather like Lizzie Siddall), the Black Prince (also reminiscent of Lizzie Siddall, despite being clothed in black armour), and those girls besieged by Indian mutineers at Lucknow (decidedly Siddall-like too), calling 'Dinna ye hear them?'

A new edition appeared in the 1920s with additional chapters covering the First World War and the League of Nations, and there was a third edition in 1953. Each was reprinted many times, but by the late 1970s received opinion had it that the book was politically equivalent to Baden- (or Enoch) Powell: beyond the pale. Copies were scarce, however; people kept them – in cupboards, perhaps, never in the drawing-room. (Or were they afraid to take them to Oxfam?) In 1988 I found a copy of the 1920s edition high on a shelf in a second-hand bookshop and furtively bought it. As a bookseller I had often heard it referred to in wistful tones, for there was a dearth of history books for children, and I suppose I thought I would sell it on. But I remembered it with such fondness that I couldn't bear to part with it, for it seemed inconceivable that it would ever be reprinted.

Now there is an anniversary edition, produced by Galore Park and the right-wing think-tank Civitas. What has happened? Is this a

'Dinna ye hear them?' Lizzie Siddall lookalikes besieged at Lucknow

putsch? An attempt by diehard crazies to repaint the map pink, force us unwillingly to church, take the vote from women? Intrigued, I asked my 10-year-old daughter Flora to read it (for a consideration) and to compare notes after I had read it again myself.

The first thing to say is that, despite the consideration (Fashion Pollies multiplying in her mind's eye), Flora enjoyed it. The narrative voice is robust and energetic: people are wise or foolish, brave or cowardly; monarchs are loved or hated; and children are assumed to appreciate adventure stories (don't we all?). In her 1905 introduction, Henrietta Marshall tells us that she hopes her book will sit on a shelf 'beside *Robinson Crusoe* and *A Noah's Ark Geography*' rather than with school books: 'When you find out how much has been left untold . . . do not be cross, but remember . . . that I was not trying to teach you, but only to tell a story'. Later, in the context of Merlin bringing over the stones for Stonehenge from Ireland, we read, 'Most people say this is a fairytale . . . I dare say they are right, but fairy tales are very interesting.' It is surprising to see her so unapologetic about subordinating facts to her narrative, and interesting to see why: the point is that at one time people must have believed such stories to be true. There is a hint already that the book is as much about the structure of our beliefs as it is a simple chronicle.

But isn't this just the objection? Under the guise of all those tales of romance and derring-do, isn't the author purveying pernicious doctrines to innocent children – Empire, patriarchy, militarism and all that other redundant claptrap? I tentatively asked Flora (who goes to a thoroughly multicultural school; thirty-three first languages, they say) if she thought the book was 'unfair' to anyone. She pronounced that it was a bit unfair to the Danes and the Normans. What about the account of the Indian Mutiny? 'Well, she doesn't explain the Indian point of view very well: the Indians', said Flora, 'were fighting for their freedom.' What about the Maori? 'She doesn't dislike the Maori in the way she dislikes Ethelred the Unready, but she doesn't think it's right that they are cannibals.' Hard to argue with that, I thought, and moved on to the American question. 'She thinks it was a shame we lost America, but she admires the Americans for standing up for themselves.'

So where are all those devilish attitudes with which I have supposedly corrupted my daughter? Turning back to my old edition, in a chapter concerning the Reform Act and the Abolition of Slavery, I find this: 'In the old, rough, wild days no one cared about the sufferings of these poor, black people. They were only niggers.' The use of the word 'niggers' is distracting here because it is nowadays considered offensive regardless of its context. Its removal leaves a passage that is (and always was) unequivocal in approving the abolition of slavery. More awkward are one or two matters in the Antipodes.

Marshall says, 'although they were cannibals, the Maoris were not nearly such a low kind of savage as the Australian, and a missionary called Marsden, hearing about these islands and their people, made up his mind to teach them to be Christian'. The dated, objectionable racial characterizations have been excised from the new edition but Marsden remains, although many would now dispute his virtues.

It is irritating to find no note on the textual changes in the new edition, but I don't believe there are many. They are limited to cases of historical inaccuracy, such as the location of the Stone of Scone, which was removed from Westminster to Scotland in 1996, and to instances where language has become dated by changed attitudes, in particular towards race; that is to say where Marshall's words carry implications for modern readers that divert us from her point. But it should not be supposed that the book has been purged of value judgements. It remains full of them. They invigorate the narrative and are integral to its appeal for children (think of Harry Potter). Moreover, it is striking how different these values are from those which the book was supposed to express in the days of its disgrace. Time and again the author takes the side of those who champion the principles of no taxation without representation, no imprisonment without trial, and freedom of worship. It is no wonder that Ethelred is a baddy, because he taxed the people without their consent to pay off the Danes. Richard III is evil because he shoved the poor princes in prison and murdered them without giving them a trial. Jenny Geddes is described as striking a blow for freedom.

I am told that Civitas wanted to publish *Our Island Story* because it gives a good account of how Britain has struggled for its institutions. The idea is that children should learn to value these institutions and not take them for granted. At a time when even habeas corpus is threatened, republication of the book seems more like an embrace of liberalism than a retreat to neo-imperialism. If Flora thinks that Marshall does not properly explain that the Indians were fighting for their freedom during the Indian Mutiny, it is partly because reading Marshall has prompted her to think that right might have been on their side. And if Marshall does not describe the savagery with which the British put down the Mutiny, perhaps that is one of the untold stories which she hopes her readers will learn not to be cross about.

Every story Marshall chooses to tell has countervailing ones in the shadows, and simplifications are essential to history for children (and adults too). Questions about what simplifications are appropriate or helpful are highly politicized, but the result, until recently, is that very few engaging history books for children have been available, which is supremely unhelpful. Flora has emerged from this account of the Indian Mutiny with the knowledge that it happened, the feeling that violence was unfortunate and the belief that the Indians were in some way being abused in order for it to have occurred at all. This seems better than holding all learning hostage to knowing about the savage but complex aftermath, and the accompanying conviction that the British imperial enterprise was wicked. She can get there in due course, if she wants, and it is worth noting that the essence of the objection to Marshall's omission is that Flora's mind should be made up for her about events, which is precisely what Marshall does not do. A recurring point in her book is that there is more to be said on any given subject. There are always untold stories, but unless you allow events to flow as stories, no one will ever learn anything.

The determination to impose contemporary value judgements on history has been extraordinarily successful in stifling children's interest in it for a generation. It is a great educational and cultural tragedy, and the lack of decent history books for children is symptomatic of it. It has now been addressed by the publication of Rebecca Fraser's excellent *A People's History of Britain* and Robert Lacey's two-volume *Tales from British History*. The success of the reissue of *Our Island Story* suggests a further desire to alter the trend. It has already sold 30,000 copies and sponsorship is in place to provide a copy to any UK primary school that asks for it.

It is cheering too to note the success of Ernst Gombrich's *A Little History of the World.* First published in Vienna in 1936, it was translated into many languages but never into English. Despite the vast later success of *The Story of Art,* the author felt that the English view of history was too Anglocentric to appreciate his early book. However, towards the end of his life he came to believe that there was a shift in perception and that his first book could be adapted for English children. Intriguingly, it was not published by his usual publisher Phaidon but by Yale, and it is a superb work, suitable for adults who have been robbed of a historical education as well as for children. (It is also beautifully illustrated by Clifford Harper, one of whose images is reproduced below and another on p.4.)

Mesopotamia, Ancient Egypt, the Persians, Greece, Rome, India, China, Christianity, the Arab world and Islam, the Mongols, America . . . and then Europe, the Age of Chivalry, the Renaissance and the Reformation . . . it is amazing how wide-ranging Gombrich is, and effortlessly so. The narrative is directed at children – 'I imagine you'd like to know exactly what happened to Gautama [the Buddha] as he sat under that fig tree'; 'When I was a schoolboy, China was to us, as it were, "at the other end of the world"' – but he is kindly without ever being patronizing. He shows what a colossal wealth of interesting ideas, events, phenomena and objects are to be found in the past. There is a sense of generosity, of a man sharing what he knows with others, telling a story, awakening interest. He

pays his readers a compliment by assuming that they will follow him, and respectfully prompts them to ask questions for themselves.

There has been one fascinating, vitriolic attack on the book – not for what the author says, but for what he does not say. The absence of any condemnation of Stalin, and Communism in general, has been perceived by one right-wing critic to be a culpable failure. That Gombrich's wise and civilized book has been described as if it were a Marxist-Leninist tract will astonish anyone who reads it. Once again, an untold story is being used to stop children from being told any stories at all. But children will learn to interpret things for themselves, and they are not necessarily as stupid as we try, with all our good intentions, to make them.

JOHN DE FALBE has been selling books at John Sandoe's in Chelsea for almost 20 years. He is the author of two novels, *The Glass Night* and *The Bequest*, and he reviews regularly.

Uncle Solly's World

TARQUIN HALL

A few years ago, I was living in an attic above a Bangladeshi sweatshop on Brick Lane in London's East End. To escape its mice-ridden confines (not to mention my landlord, Mr Ali, who was forever coming upstairs to help himself to my booze and watch cricket on my TV), I would escape to the Whitechapel Library around the corner.

I found myself in good company. Nearly everyone in the reference section was trying to escape something. The tramps sought refuge from the English weather; the OAPs from the tedium of retirement; young Bangladeshis studying GCSEs from the cramped confines of their council flats. In the middle of unruly Whitechapel, the library was a sanctuary. And just as the poet Isaac Rosenberg had once feasted on literature, philosophy and economic and political theory in the place the East End Jews called 'The University of the Poor', so young immigrants now studied for their Open University degrees, trying to earn a one-way ticket out of the ghetto.

I joined them, making use of the library to educate myself about the East End. I had never set foot in the area before; my childhood was spent in leafy SW13 and most of my adult life in places like Pakistan. But, returning to England unemployed and broke in the winter of 1999, I found myself washed up on Brick Lane. My first few weeks in the attic above the sweatshop had brought on feverish culture shock. But since then, I'd managed to recover and had begun to

---

Emanuel Litvinoff's *Journey Through a Small Planet* (1972) has been published in various editions, none of which is now in print. However, copies can be obtained through second-hand bookshops or via the Internet.

explore the neighbourhood – on foot and through the library's stacks.

My favourite desk stood between tall shelves crammed with Bengali, Somali and Urdu classics, which had replaced the Yiddish collection. Here, I read my way through all the history books and memoirs on east London. These included an extensive collection of 'Cor-Blimey-There's-Nothing-Like-a-Knees-Up!' autobiographies, and the 'Dodgy Geezers that I 'ave Known' genre, but thankfully, there were more thoughtful accounts on offer. Among them, I discovered Emanuel Litvinoff's *Journey Through a Small Planet* – a masterpiece that rivals George Orwell's best non-fiction. In fact it was to inspire me to write my own account of life on Brick Lane.

Litvinoff's refreshingly realistic view of the East End of his childhood in the 1920s and '30s rang especially true. It was no Cockney paradise full of chirpy Pearlies; nor does he portray it as an immigrant Shangri-La. His world was filthy and overpopulated, packed with sweatshops that gave off a 'stench of overcrowding and decay'. Nowhere does he express a hint of sentimentality for the ghetto, even though, in his lifetime, he would watch it disappear.

What Litvinoff does celebrate, however, are the characters – all of them ordinary men and women – who inhabited his world and whose idiosyncrasies made it so colourful. Indeed, for an autobiography, the book contains very little of the author. We learn only that he was a typical teenager, full of dreams and hormones, prone to falling in with the wrong crowd; and that, upon reaching manhood and wanting to become a writer, he penned his first novel on scraps of paper. Instead, each chapter is dedicated to the daily struggles of relatives, friends, neighbours and the occasional enemy – all of them deliciously flawed.

First we come to know Mark Golombek, a Ukrainian clothes presser and revolutionary, who would insert leaflets inside soldiers' uniforms that read, 'DOWN WITH BLOODTHIRSTY CAPITALISM!' Next we meet Litvinoff's mother, Rosa, who fled Russia for London where her husband left her 'pregnant and twenty-two, with nothing but three children, a sewing machine and her skill in dressmaking'. Then we're introduced to Mickey Lerner, who was regularly caned at school for refusing to sing 'Land of Hope and Glory'. Finally, there's the belle of the neighbourhood, Fanya Ziegelbaum. Seduced by Herschel Rosenheim, a touring American actor, she's forced to have an abortion at Fat Yetta's backstreet clinic.

Litvinoff developed a justifiable contempt for some. 'Fathers – what I'd seen of them – were not much of a bargain,' he writes. 'They stank of sweat and strong tobacco; [and] when they grabbed you in an unwanted embrace their rough beards rasped your skin.' From an early age, Litvinoff lived in constant fear that his mother would marry again. He managed to see off one suitor, a Mister Paisky, who had a smile that revealed 'a gold tooth in the ruined cavern of his mouth'. But eventually, the young man's worst fears came true in the form of Uncle Solly. A smooth talker who carried a Malacca cane, he claimed to have 'killed Germans in Gallipoli and France, prospected for diamonds, [and] strode once with the same nonchalance amongst the Kaffirs of the African veldt'. Like all the others, Uncle Solly turned out to be trouble. An impulsive gambler who kept Rosa in a permanent state of pregnancy, he spent most of his evenings lying on the sofa 'half undressed, scratching reflectively at his hairy armpit and dribbling smoke from a hand-rolled cigarette'.

Litvinoff's home was a dilapidated tenement building filled with the pervasive stench of cats, where neighbours banged broomsticks on each other's walls and ceilings. He was never in any doubt that he wanted to escape – and he was not alone. 'We were all dreamers,' he writes, 'each convinced it was his destiny to grow rich, or famous, or change the world to a marvellous place of freedom and justice. No wonder so many of us were haunted by bitterness, failure and despair.'

That collage of dreams and failure, destiny and despair remains etched on the East End's human landscape. The Welfare State ensures people no longer starve to death; and young girls aren't sold under the railway arches as they were in Dr Barnado's day. But still, the borough of Tower Hamlets, encompassing the East End proper, remains the poorest in Britain. Thousands of families still live six to a room in crumbling estates, poverty and unemployment are rife, violent crime is rampant and heroin is the new gin.

The parallels between the old Jewish East End and the new Muslim-dominated one don't end there. The Bangladeshis, who number around 60,000, have learned to live with racism just as the Jews did. Like their predecessors, most first-generation Bangladeshis have clung together, mirroring Litvinoff's old tenement building – 'a village in miniature, a place of ingathered exiles who supplemented their Jewish speech with phrases in Russian, Polish or Lithuanian'.

This insular existence trapped many of Litvinoff's generation, and today, some young British Bangladeshis find themselves caught in the same culture gap. You can see them on street corners dealing in drugs and fighting turf wars. Others have turned to Wahabi-inspired Islamic fundamentalism, previously unknown in the Bengali tradition. They condone violence against the British state and aspire to fill the shoes of Litvinoff's childhood friend 'Gurevich', a Marxist revolutionary who planted a bomb on Tower Bridge.

In short, the immigrant gestation period is no less painful today than it was in the 1920s – or perhaps at any time in the East End's past. But *Journey Through a Small Planet* offers hope. Although Litvinoff himself felt disenfranchised from his family, community and religion – just as he did from the wider Anglo-Saxon society – he, like tens of thousands of other Jews who populated east London between the 1880s and 1960s, did manage to escape. And, just as the Glaxos and Gestetners achieved success, Litvinoff also realized his dream, transforming himself into a novelist and poet.

TARQUIN HALL is the author of *Salaam Brick Lane: A Year in the New East End*, published last year. He lived on Brick Lane for two and a half years but has since gone up-market and moved to Hackney.

Top Dog

CAROLINE CHAPMAN

As the years advance I've become increasingly aware of the books I read as a child that have exerted an influence on my life. Would I have just returned from my fourth tramp through the African bush, for example, had my imagination not been fired by a vivid account of the bond that developed between a man and his dog as they hunted big game in the South African veld? Among the many seeds sown in my childhood, *Jock of the Bushveld* fell on richly fertile ground.

In the late nineteenth century the discovery of gold in the Transvaal brought fortune hunters from every corner of the globe. Among them was a young man named Percy FitzPatrick who had abandoned a dull job to seek adventure in the gold fields. But work was scarce; after attempts at prospecting and store-keeping, he became a transport-rider. At that time supplies for the mines were carried overland from the coast: huge spans of fourteen or sixteen oxen hauled heavily laden wagons along rutted tracks, through thorny scrub and grassland, across broad rivers, through swamps infested by tsetse fly, and finally up a precipitous escarpment to the mining camps beyond. Apart from essentials such as tea, sugar and salt, the wagons brought only those goods that fetched high prices in the gold fields. To provide meat for his team of drivers, the transport-rider had to hunt for it along the way. For this task, a good dog was essential.

Percy FitzPatrick's *Jock of the Bushveld* (1907) now appears to be out of print, but copies of various editions are available from second-hand bookshops or www.abe.com.

Enter Jock, the runt of a litter of six puppies born to a mean but plucky bitch named Jess. With his crumpled little face, bandy legs and stump of a tail, he was dubbed 'the Rat' and threatened with extinction. But the Rat's tenacity, courage and touching dignity had won Percy's respect and he decided to adopt him. He began the dog's education at once, training him to obey his every command. (I was so inspired by this description of canine obedience that I tried out Percy's methods on my recalcitrant poodle puppy with, I must confess, a resounding lack of success.)

The Rat had soon grown into a handsome dog with a coat of burnished gold and bright dark eyes which turned to beady black when he was roused. (A watercolour of Jock by E. Caldwell, together with many brilliant line drawings, adorns my 1911 copy of the book, and has remained an indelible image from my childhood.) It was time to put the months of training to the test. So with Jock at his heels, Percy set off into the sun-baked veld carrying only a rifle, a cartridge belt and a water-bottle. He was as much a beginner as Jock, and during their early hunts together they both made mistakes. But Percy was left in no doubt that in Jock he had found a dog of incomparable worth, a fact proved time and again during the many thrilling and often dangerous encounters with big game which are so vividly described in the book. Jock's skill and intelligence enabled him to outmanoeuvre a wounded animal, and once he had brought it down and fastened his teeth into part of its anatomy, nothing would induce him to let go. Despite being tossed and shaken like a rat, thrashed along the ground, struck at by razor-sharp hooves and wicked horns, he hung on grimly until Percy was able to deliver the *coup de grâce*.

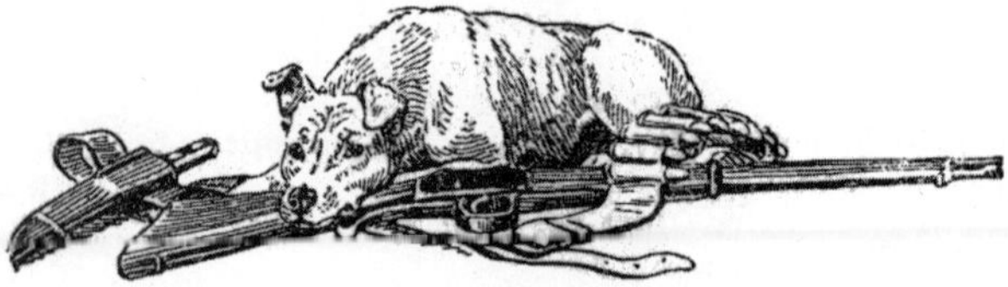

Some may argue that the contest was an unfair one: that a man with a gun and a clever dog exercised an unfair advantage over his quarry. But the veld was vast and the game elusive, swift of foot, occasionally downright hostile and frequently invisible. Percy would often know by Jock's behaviour that they were within yards of an animal, but so perfect was its camouflage that he was quite unable to see it: 'Twice Jock slowly turned his head and looked into my eyes, and I felt keenly the sense of hopeless inferiority.' This blindness would persist until the swish of a tail or the flick of an ear brought the animal into sharp relief.

Sometimes a routine hunt would take an unexpected turn. During one long and tortuous pursuit of a wounded buck, Percy became hopelessly lost, a mistake which in the immensity of the veld – then still home to lion and leopard – could have been fatal. On another occasion, a stealthy stalk along a dry watercourse landed him in the middle of a herd of impala. 'There were a few minutes of complete bewilderment, a scene of the wildest confusion' before the terrified animals began to leap in every direction. In 'the whirlpool of racing and plunging' beasts, Percy and Jock became separated and Percy had to return to camp alone, leaving his beloved dog exposed to the perils of the night.

The veld itself could be treacherous: Percy and some friends once found themselves trapped by a bush fire in a narrow gorge. In desperation, they burnt an area of grass large enough to afford them protection and then retreated to its centre, Percy clutching Jock in his arms. 'Then down on the wings of the wind came the other fire, and before it fled every living thing', their staring eyes and frenzied forms glimpsed fleetingly through the smoke – among them a black mamba, the most deadly of snakes, which 'came sailing out of the yellow grasses . . . and passed between us, giving a quick, chilly, beady look at each – pitiless and hateful – and one hiss as the slithering tongue shot out'. Fainting with heat and exhaustion, Percy records his intense relief when 'our burn divided [the fire] as an island splits the flood, and it swept along our flanks in two great walls of living, leaping, roaring flame . . .'

Percy's career as a transport-rider ended abruptly with the death of his entire team of oxen from disease. Years later, he relived his time in the veld by recounting his adventures with Jock to his children. Hearing him tell the stories, a family friend – Rudyard Kipling – persuaded him to commit them to paper. Thus was born this classic among animal stories, a book declared by Theodore Roosevelt to be 'the best and truest story of a dog that I have ever read, and I think I have read them all'.

CAROLINE CHAPMAN's first biography, of Lady Elizabeth Foster, was published in 2002. Since then she has been searching for a new subject. Any ideas?

A Fine Burgundy

MARK VALENTINE

It is a hundred years since Baroness Orczy gave us her splendid swashbuckler *The Scarlet Pimpernel* (1905). One great admirer of the book is Peter Vansittart, who has himself written many well-received historical novels, and others with contemporary themes. The Sir Percy Blakeney type – insouciant, raffish, always liable to turn up unexpectedly in tight corners – is one he much admires. Yet, though relishing the Baroness's work, he was also determined, as an emerging author in the 1950s, to do some something new with the historical novel, to move it on from 'gadzookery', or what Robert Louis Stevenson called, half-affectionately, 'tushery'.

This he first succeeded in doing with his fine novel set in a (lightly disguised) medieval Burgundy, *The Tournament* (1958). His great achievement is to take us into the completely different way of thinking of the men and women of those times; their superstitions and certainties, their rituals and fetishes and taboos. As he pointed out in an essay heralding his aims in the novel, even such primary things as colour had different meanings for them which were 'bewilderingly complex; the medievals gave each colour heraldic, moral, magical, religious, strategic meanings, often contradictory'. With quick, deft imagery he conjures up not how things might seem to us from the distance of our own time, but how they would have been seen then. The effect is unusual and arresting; he is so swift-footed, his prose so teeming with curious detail, that we want constantly to stop and

---

Peter Vansittart, *The Tournament* (1958)
Peter Owen · Hb · 224pp · £14.95 · ISBN 0720606160

reflect on what we are reading. Here is an example of his gift for poetic brevity and his eye for myth:

> Beacons had been lit on the low surrounding hills and on the walls of distant castles, flickering palely in the sunlight like the Forlorn Fires burned by those who had been enchanted; and in the fields, behind the gesticulating mobs, garlands had even been placed on the sheep's skulls stuck on poles to protect the land against lightning. It was also said that the young men had swarmed the woods and slain a wren that wore a golden crown.

For a long time I have found this strange, glinting book a source of fascination, drawn by its extravagant colours certainly, but also by the wayward personalities in it: the Duke, his fool, his courtiers, his moody heir, his estranged wife, his credulous yet practical peasants. So when I got the chance to visit Peter Vansittart, now in his eighties, in his Suffolk cottage, I was keen to find out more about the inspiration behind it. I asked what had drawn him to the theme of the novel, which might seem somewhat recondite. He told me: 'I was very interested in the fact that Burgundy had no distinctive boundaries and so it had to depend for its existence on bluff, on propaganda, magnificence. The Duchy was so extravagant that it would be difficult to exaggerate it. I read in a history that the Duke of Burgundy had been insulted by another prince, a challenge had been issued, and all sorts of preparations were made. But, the paragraph concluded simply, "The tournament did not take place." And I suddenly realized it had never been intended to take place, it was just a gesture, all part of an empty ritual. That was like turning a key in the lock; there was my book.'

It is not quite so easy to find the key to Peter Vansittart. Born in 1920, into a family with its own share of eminence, he noted that his father's death certificate gave 'Occupation – Gentleman', but said he knew little else about him (he died before Peter was born). Something of that elusiveness has descended on the son too. He is

'How sad the sound of a hunting horn in the woods.' By James Nunn

quicker to tell of the books he enjoys and the fellow-authors he has known than to talk of himself, and one only gradually gathers a sense of him. Courteous, hospitable, gently satirical, alert to irony, full of curious lore, he is like one of the courtiers in his book, where indeed he would not be the only modern, as I was soon to discover.

But first we spoke of another major theme in the novel, one that takes it into more sombre terrain. The Duke, for all his pomp, is a ruler, with responsibilities, with hard decisions to make, a steward of lives. This becomes increasingly understood by him as the story progresses. What recalls him to his duty was not hard to imagine, said Vansittart: 'When I was about 18, I read books on the Black Death and secreted away one or two odd little details – for instance, that doctors wore beaks like birds and the beaks were filled with herbs to protect them. If you got the Black Death, you would try to infect family and friends so they would join you in the after-life.'

Here, then, were the beginnings of the novel; all his life, Peter Vansittart has been an assiduous and retentive reader, and a habitual note-taker, and he makes his books like a mosaic, piece by piece, deftly placing a vivid symbol here, a bizarre belief there. 'It wasn't that I did any research specifically for the book,' he told me, 'I had just absorbed so much from my reading. Occasionally I would verify things after I had done the writing, but not before or during. One knows more than one realizes. You start writing, and everything falls into place. I've always thought the more research you do, the worse the novel. I remember reading as a boy Conan Doyle's introduction to *The White Company* in which he says he read over sixty books to prepare for writing it. Even then, I couldn't help thinking it would have been a better novel if he hadn't read any.'

Certainly *The Tournament* does not read like a brigade of text-books forced into fiction, as some historical novels do. For Vansittart's characters are richly human, with their follies and foibles, their great weaknesses and little greatnesses. How had he achieved that? Though never in the literary mainstream, in the 1950s he was part of a circle of eccentric individuals whose traits he found irresistible: and, he told me, they all found their way into his book. Philip Toynbee, author of the experimental Holy Grail novel, *Tea with Mrs Goodman*, was one; he became the Duke's heir, brilliant, petulant, proud but tainted, 'a quivering hound on his leash'. Stephen Spender is there as the Chevalier Stephen, the Duke's right-hand man, a brooding, elliptical poet, whose satire is said to have lamed a knight; the philosopher A. J. Ayer appears as the Chancellor, Lord Estrienne, sardonic, saturnine, tilting at the Church: 'It has always seemed to me disturbing, Your Grace, and also, perhaps, significant, that while we are permitted to hear the words of our Blessed Master, we shall never know the tone of voice in which he deigned to utter them.'

Did they recognize themselves? 'Oddly, no,' Peter Vansittart replied. 'Of course I couldn't have got away with it in a modern novel as that would have been too obvious: but a medieval court was an ideal chance to portray them without much fear of detection.'

Quite apart from his successful use of myth and imagery, and his engaging characters, there is something in the prose style of *The Tournament*, some convincing quality that seems to speak in the very tongue and timbre of the times in which it is set. I couldn't put my finger on this, until its author enlightened me: 'I was playing Flemish and Burgundian music while I was writing it, so that vaguely the rhythms of the music might enter the rhythms of the prose, might summon up court ritual, dirges, processions, hunting calls. There is a line of Alfred de Vigny; "God! How sad the sound of a hunting horn in the woods." That stuck in my mind. It summoned up the world of the Burgundian tapestries, which I tried to recreate.'

The Tournament was by no means the last impetus he gave to the under-regarded historical novel. In *The Friends of God* (1963), he wrote with dramatic, unflinching clarity of the brutal world of the Anabaptists, sixteenth-century German heretics. *The Death of Robin Hood* (1981) won praise from Alan Hollinghurst: 'highly original . . . a teeming, vivid, unruly fairground . . . jostling with brilliant detail and palpable immediacy'. In this novel, and in others, Vansittart was one of the first to work with resonances across time: 'I've always believed that although human behaviour changes, human nature does not. We will always build the same images, the same archetypes. So for the writer the interest is in showing how these emerge in different historical times. This is central to what I like writing about. In *Lancelot* (1978), for example, set in early, post-Roman England, you get a sudden glimpse of Hermann Goering, then of Robespierre. I try to show that there is always a sort of continuum. We cannot escape it, and it is there to be seen, behind all our history.'

His most recent novel, *Hermes in Paris* (2000), is another fine exemplification of this theme, with an avatar of the ancient god of thieves and trickery and illusions at play in the French capital during the Second Empire; a Fabergé egg of a novel, one critic called it, as brilliant and jewelled. This was the twenty-sixth of his novels, half of which have been published by his staunch independent publisher

Peter Owen. He has also written several highly enjoyable literary memoirs, a number of acclaimed histories or biographies (most recently of John Paul Jones, the American buccaneer), several original anthologies and three books of tales for children.

Though none of these have become bestsellers, I am far from alone in appreciating his work. A. S. Byatt has called him quite simply 'a wonderful novelist and storyteller . . . brilliant, unforgettable', while a guide to twentieth-century literature has rightly noted that he 'has almost single-handedly redeemed the historical novel from its middle-brow reputation'.

The author himself seems sanguine about his lack of a popular readership. 'At least I don't have to worry about disappointing my readers, because there aren't any, or there are hardly any. It allows me to go my own way. Had I written, say, *Lucky Jim*, I would have been restricted in what I might do next.' He was only once briefly convinced that wider acclaim might come his way: 'When I wrote *Orders of Chivalry* (1956), it got a marvellous review from Dorothy Parker: "The only novel that has made me howl with laughter at 2 o'clock in the morning." Well, I thought I might almost get a mortgage with that sort of praise, but of course it didn't make the slightest difference.'

It is not easy to find the work of Peter Vansittart, and when you do, you may take a little while to adjust to such succinct, sustained intelligence, such a personal and peculiar style, such singular mastery both of the undercurrents of history and of the telling details of the everyday. But then you will soon be in earnest quest of the rest.

MARK VALENTINE has been described by the *Independent* as 'a microbiologist of literary fauna' for his keen interest in overlooked writers. He has written a biography of the Welsh author and mystic Arthur Machen, and introductions to works by J. Meade Falkner, William Sansom, L. P. Hartley and others, as well as two volumes of mystery stories.

Race of Ghosts

PATRICK DENMAN FLANERY

A few years ago, I spent a week in County Galway at a country house hotel popular with fishermen during the high season, and with eccentrics in every other. I found myself in the company of a fragile lady novelist, an unladylike sculptor on the hunt for 'famine artefacts', and an ungentlemanly film-maker, drunkenly mourning the fact that his wife had run off to the Amazon jungle with a crackpot shaman who prospered on the moral failings of rich Americans. I bonded with the lady novelist over books and a mutual antipathy for another guest, a white Zimbabwean recently exiled to Belfast, who pursued us both, apparently in the hope of some sordid thrashing between the freezing sheets. As the Zimbabwean appeared to have an allergy to thought and silence, I took refuge in the library, reading, for the first time, Evelyn Waugh's *Put Out More Flags*.

Preoccupied with the 'Phoney War', from declaration to the fall of France, or what Waugh described as the 'Great Bore War', *Put Out More Flags* was his sixth novel, and although it was a great success on first publication in 1942, it seems to be one of his few novels that people don't know today. Waugh readers tend to fall into two camps, usually on either side of *Brideshead Revisited* (1945), with some reading only the 'mature' books, others sticking fiercely to the early comedies. *Put Out More Flags* is perhaps under-loved because it falls,

---

Evelyn Waugh, *Put Out More Flags* (1942)
Penguin · Pb · 240pp · £11.99 · ISBN 0141184019
Marie-Jacqueline Lancaster, *Brian Howard: A Portrait in Failure* (1968)
Timewell Press · Pb · 400pp · £14.99 · ISBN 185725211X

both chronologically and stylistically, between these two recognizable periods in Waugh's fiction.

Like *Vile Bodies*, the novel consists of a series of loosely linked episodes, following the lives of half a dozen characters but focusing on Ambrose Silk, a gay Jewish 'aesthete' writer, and Basil Seal, the irrepressible rake last seen innocently eating his girlfriend at a cannibal feast in *Black Mischief* (1932). It is Basil Seal, 'wayward and graceless and grossly disappointing', a man 'whose unaccountable taste for low company had led him into so many vexatious scrapes', who provides the book's best comic interludes, and the thread which stitches the stories together. Tempering wry comedy with a reflection of Waugh's first experience of war, *Put Out More Flags* contains a strong hint of the accomplished war writing that reached maturity in *The Sword of Honour* trilogy, his last work of fiction. Reviewing the book in the *New York Times* in 1942, John Chamberlain ungenerously likened its style to 'the wicked Saki . . . trying to make his peace with Hugh Walpole'. This is most unfair; rather, it is a novel that reflects the slow settling of sobriety on a largely superficial society awakened to the realities of war.

Waugh himself called it a 'minor work', one he 'dashed off to occupy a tedious voyage' home from active service in the summer of 1941. 'Minor' is perhaps a rare moment of false modesty on Waugh's part. *Put Out More Flags* is a book of 'good bits' such as a 'half incestuous relationship' between Basil and his sister, Barbara, who is the billeting officer for her district and wife of Freddy Sothill.

Barbara believes a war is just what her brother needs to give himself some direction: 'He's not meant for peace . . . He's always been a soldier manqué.' Unlike most men of his class, and indeed unlike his brother-in-law, Basil never bothered to join the Territorial Army or the Yeomanry. An 'obstreperous minority of one in a world of otiose civilians', Basil has clear ideas about what kind of war he wants: 'I want to be one of those people one heard about in 1919; the hard-faced men who did well out of the war.' As everyone scrambles to find something remotely official to keep them occupied, Basil half expects to be summoned to work for the Ministry of Intelligence. When no such invitation arrives, and it becomes clear that no other position is going to present itself (at least no position that Basil would condescend to accept), he retreats to Barbara and Freddy's country house, where his sister is saddled with three impossibly horrid evacuee children, Doris, Mickey and Marlene Connolly.

Doris, the eldest, takes a grotesque fancy to Basil, flirting and begging him to pull her hair when she isn't 'rubbing herself on a pilaster like a cow on a stump'. Basil sees an opportunity, and armed with Barbara's address book, sets about systematically placing the children in the homes of the people least likely to want them but most able to afford them. When their temporary hosts can take no more, he goads them into paying to billet the Connollys elsewhere, making himself a tidy profit.

Basil's first victims are an elderly artistic couple, Mr and Mrs Harkness, who have advertised for other 'elderly or artistic people wishing to avoid war worries' to join them as paying guests, 'highest references given and expected'. Hiding the Connollys in his car, Basil approaches the wisteria-covered Old Mill and allows the unwitting Harknesses to show him round their corner of paradise. Mr Harkness is keen to emphasize his home's quiet delights: in summer, there are 'meals under the old mulberry tree' and 'Music. Every week we have chamber music.' All these accumulated 'imponderabilia', Mr Harkness insists, 'have their market value', of precisely six guineas a week.

Basil seizes the moment, and Waugh's description of the assault is perfection:

> This was the time for the grenade he had been nursing ever since he opened the little, wrought-iron gate and put his hand to the wrought-iron bell-pull. 'We pay eight shillings and sixpence a week,' he said . . . Here it comes. Bang! 'Perhaps I

should have told you at once. I am the billeting officer. I've three children for you in the car outside.'

It was magnificent. It was war.

The Harknesses protest: 'you've seen for yourself this lovely old house and the kind of life we live here. Don't you feel that there is something different here, something precious that could so easily be killed?' Basil is unswayable and, inevitably, a heavy snowfall cuts off the Old Mill for eight days, stranding the couple with the children. When the roads are cleared, Harkness, a ruined man, comes to plead with Basil for mercy:

'I thought of giving them weed-killer,' said Mr Harkness wistfully.

'Yes,' said Basil, 'that would be one way. Do you think Marlene could keep it down?'

'Or hanging.'

'Come, come, Mr Harkness, this is mere wishful thinking. We must be more practical.'

'Everything I've thought of has had Death in it; ours or theirs.'

Harkness finally agrees to pay Basil £30, and the Connollys are once again his to exploit. The scam hits a snag, however, when Basil tries it on a Mr Todhunter, the billeting officer for the neighbouring district. Forced to explain the mechanics of the scheme to Todhunter, Basil sells him the Connollys and decamps to London. Pretending to be a member of the fictitious MI13, he then bluffs his way into the War Office, where he persuades the Assistant Deputy Director Internal Security, Colonel Plum, to give him a uniform and an unpaid job as a Second Lieutenant in the General Service List, assigned to monitor communists and ferret out fascists.

Running parallel to Basil's exploits is Waugh's surprisingly tender treatment of Ambrose Silk. Modelled on Brian Howard, the Old Etonian poet and notorious aesthete who had a long-term German boyfriend (and whose own story is the subject of Marie-Jacqueline

Lancaster's *Brian Howard: Portrait of a Failure*), Ambrose is the 'sole representative of Atheism in the religious department' at the Ministry of Information, and editor of the *Ivory Tower*, a highbrow literary review modelled on the *Yellow Book*. Ambrose is also the magazine's sole contributor, hiding his authorship behind the unlikely pseudonyms 'Hucklebury Squib' and 'Tom Barebones-Abraham'. The centrepiece of the first issue is 'Monument to a Spartan', a fifty-page homage to Hans, Ambrose's German ex-boyfriend.

Basil, an old but by no means faithful friend of Ambrose's, sees in *Ivory Tower* another opportunity for his own advancement. He persuades Ambrose to edit 'Monument to a Spartan' so that it reads, without its author realizing it, as a paean to the Hitler Youth. Basil passes an edited copy to Colonel Plum, who orders Ambrose's arrest, believing him to be a fifth-columnist. Feeling a twinge of delayed remorse, Basil disguises Ambrose as a Jesuit priest and sends him, on a stolen passport, into exile in Ireland, while Basil takes up residence in Ambrose's abandoned flat.

In his dedication to Randolph Churchill, Waugh concedes that the book deals with 'a race of ghosts', characters who 'are no longer contemporary in sympathy' but survive 'delightfully in holes and corners and, like everyone else,' are 'disturbed in their habits by the rough intrusion of current history'. The currents of history have a way of intruding roughly into settled habits, and *Put Out More Flags* offers an often hilarious reminder that one must laugh even amid dark days, even when a society finds itself forcibly shaken into sobriety.

Waugh would perhaps be satisfied to know that his race of ghosts still survives in holes and corners, not least in country house hotels in the west of Ireland, where, like Ambrose Silk, lady novelists, ungentlemanly film-makers and ex-Zimbabweans seek a harbour from the currents of contemporary history.

PATRICK DENMAN FLANERY is finishing a doctorate on Evelyn Waugh at Oxford. The currents of history alarm him.

In Search of Shangri-La

JOHN HAMMOND

I first discovered James Hilton's *Lost Horizon* as an adolescent, when I came across a hardback copy in a secondhand bookshop marked at one shilling and ninepence (8p in today's money). It was published in Macmillan's Cottage Library and I can still remember its nice clear typeface, the feel of its rounded corners, and the slight browning of the pages which added a nostalgic charm. As soon as I read the opening sentence I was hooked:

> Cigars had burned low, and we were beginning to sample the disillusionment that usually afflicts old school friends who meet again as men and find themselves with less in common than they used to think . . .

At the time I enjoyed it simply as an adventure story, but each subsequent reading has revealed new layers of meaning. Over the years I have come back to this beguiling novel many times, and however often I do so, I never tire of it. It has become part of my inner world.

Lost Horizon, which was first published in 1933, tells the story of a group of four people – a diplomat, his assistant, a missionary and an American financier – who find themselves in the Afghan city of Kabul (disguised by Hilton as Baskul) when civil war breaks out. They attempt to escape by plane to India but the plane is hijacked and they are taken instead to a mysterious lamasery – the Shangri-La of the title – in a remote area of Tibet.

James Hilton, *Lost Horizon* (1933)
Summersdale · Pb · £7.99 · 256pp · ISBN 1840243538

This is their magical first glimpse of it:

> A group of coloured pavilions clung to the mountainside with none of the grim deliberation of a Rhineland castle, but rather with the chance delicacy of flower-petals impaled upon a crag. It was superb and exquisite . . . the feeling was only momentary, and soon merged in the deeper sensation, half mystical, half visual, of having reached at last some place that was an end, a finality.

Inside the lamasery they find a gentle, cultured community, isolated from Western civilization and determined to maintain its library and art treasures despite the gathering clouds of war. Hugh Conway, the British diplomat whose narrative forms the basis of the novel, is increasingly attracted to the calm and gentle atmosphere of Shangri-La and has many conversations with the ruler of the community, the High Lama.

Since Conway is disillusioned with his job and secretly yearns for a life of study and contemplation (he had at one time been an Oxford don) he finds the lamasery and its unhurried philosophy more and more appealing. He learns that the lamasery intends to keep him and his colleagues permanently but he dare not break this news to them at first, though he realizes they will have to know eventually. He also learns that the unique atmosphere at Shangri-La delays the ageing process and that it is not uncommon for residents to live for a century or more.

With great reluctance he ultimately decides to leave since his impetuous young colleague, Mallinson, is determined to do so and cannot attempt the difficult journey without his help. Mallinson has fallen in love with a Chinese girl, Lo-Tsen, and wishes to escape with her. (Lo-Tsen has lived at the lamasery since 1884, having lost her way in the mountains while travelling to join her betrothed: she has not aged in the interim.) The missionary and the financier are content to remain at Shangri-La, but Mallinson and Conway leave together.

They are determined to reach India and ultimately England, but their attempt has tragic consequences. The story ends with Conway making desperate efforts to find his way back to Shangri-La, leaving the question ringing in the reader's ears: 'Do you think he will ever find it?'

Such a bald summary cannot do justice to the haunting atmosphere of *Lost Horizon*. I know of no other novel that leaves the reader with such a powerful sense of loss. Some of its images remain in the mind long after one has finished reading – the journey by plane across the snow-covered mountains, the approach to Shangri-La, the meeting with the High Lama, the departure from the lamasery, the sudden ageing of Lo-Tsen. These scenes were brilliantly captured in Frank Capra's 1937 film version, starring Ronald Colman. Capra went to great lengths to ensure that the film was as technically accurate as possible and spent much time on research into Tibetan fashions, buildings and customs.

In the 1930s Tibet was virtually unknown to readers in the Western world, and Hilton's vision of this remote and idyllic civilization was fresh and exciting. Younghusband had succeeded in reaching Lhasa in 1904, but after his brief exploration Tibet was once again shrouded in mystery. A medieval theocracy surrounded by impenetrable mountain ranges, it was regarded as a lost world. Long after the publication of *Lost Horizon* Tibet continued to be largely unknown. Heinrich Harrer's classic *Seven Years in Tibet*, which includes fascinating descriptions of the country and its people in the 1940s, was not published until 1953. Tibet has, of course, been under Chinese occupation since 1950, but despite this vast tracts of the country are still inaccessible and only nominally under Chinese rule. The Kun Lun mountains, where Hilton located Shangri-La, remain to this day largely unexplored, though this vast mountain range contains peaks almost as high as Everest.

When Hilton was asked why he chose to write about such a remote civilization he replied: 'Obscure places and people have a great attraction for me and Tibet is one of the few places on earth that is still comparatively inaccessible.' Yet, ironically, Hilton himself had never visited Tibet. Instead he had immersed himself in books about the country, in particular the writings of the American explorer Joseph Rock who had travelled widely in Tibet in the 1920s and 1930s. It was Rock's vivid accounts in the *National Geographic Magazine* of lofty mountain ranges, windswept plateaux and hidden valleys that inspired Hilton to set his novel in this inhospitable terrain.

Lost Horizon was first published at a time of mounting unemployment and depression, when the Nazi regime was just beginning its programme of persecution. With its powerful anti-war message and emphasis on gentleness and compassion, the novel struck a deep chord. It won the Hawthornden prize in 1934 (the equivalent of today's Booker) and has been continuously in print on both sides of the Atlantic ever since. Hilton went on to write other best-selling novels including *Goodbye Mr Chips* and *Random Harvest*, but perhaps *Lost Horizon* made the most lasting mark. Few novels can claim to have added a new word to the English language: 'Shangri-La' has come to mean any ideal retreat from the world, and it must now be one of the most popular house names in England.

Several writers have tried their hand at writing a sequel – the film buff Leslie Halliwell with *Return to Shangri-La* in 1987, and two American writers, Eleanor Cooney and Daniel Altiery, with *Shangri-La: The Return to the World of Lost Horizon* in 1996 – but neither captures the haunting flavour of the original. The utter inaccessibility that Hilton managed to convey, the sense of something remote and beyond our reach, must surely explain the novel's lasting appeal. For most of us love a mystery.

JOHN HAMMOND has written books on Wells, Poe, Orwell, Stevenson and Defoe. He is keenly interested in the author of *Lost Horizon*, and in 2000 founded a society to promote interest in James Hilton's life and work.

Edit and Be Damned

CHARLES ELLIOTT

Editing must be one of the few professions that require no professional training. Even a plumber needs to learn how to plumb before he's allowed to attack pipes. An editor, on the other hand, just takes up his spanner and blowtorch and starts editing.

Of course there are a lot of different kinds of editors (and I've been most of them at one time or another): line editors (known in England as copy editors), newspaper editors, magazine editors, book editors. The skills involved in each case are distinctive, but they all share this same amateur, self-taught quality. Editing is something that you tend to fall into, though perhaps not entirely by accident. Editors are born, not made.

It may be worth stressing this, because editors get a lot of flak from people – especially writers – who cannot accept that anyone should be in a position to turn down a book, or correct their grammar, or in some other way act superior. They are right, nobody should be, except that's the editor's job. The truth of the matter is that most editors spend a considerable amount of psychological capital convincing themselves that their judgement is right. The position must necessarily be: I edit, therefore I am an editor. In a realm with absolutely no firm rules against which one's opinions may be measured, it's the only thing to do. Thus armed, you have at least a fighting chance of facing the world (or a writer) with confidence.

At the most basic level, line or copy editing, an editor needs a technique for judging and perhaps improving a piece of writing. My own has always been to read slowly, 'listening' for imprecision, wrong words, failure to track properly. This seems to work; a good writer sounds fine, a bad one bumpy or inept. The rhythm is wrong. It is usually pretty simple to identify the rough spots and either fix them or tell the writer to do so. (My predecessor at *Life* magazine, where I worked many years ago, had a rule of thumb for this – if a caption or a piece of text could be repaired with a pencil, fine; if you had to have recourse to a typewriter to do it, send the piece back to the writer.) But there is no way to avoid the conclusion that the procedure is hopelessly subjective, and to make it work at all you have to keep on telling yourself that your ear is incomparable.

On occasion I've had my doubts. When *Life* folded in 1972, I went to work as a book editor for the New York publisher Alfred A. Knopf. This was a fairly radical change, and I soon found out just how radical. Alistair Cooke, it seemed, was in the process of writing a book to accompany his television series *America*. The programmes would be broadcast in the autumn; it was then already March. Knopf had paid a staggering (for the time) $400,000 for the rights, and the book simply had to be published at the time of the broadcast. Alistair was still writing madly and not, it has to be said, as carefully as he might. Each week or two another handful of scruffy yellow pages would turn up in the office. Eventually a pile of these were handed to me to edit.

Having practised my trade at a place where editing was more likely to be done with a broadaxe than a scalpel, I set to work as I best knew how. I quickly saw that Cooke's copy was going to need some serious fixing, so I fixed. When I was done I had the whole thing retyped, suspecting that it might be better not to let the great man see what I'd done to his prose, and delivered it to him at the Fairmount Hotel in San Francisco where he was staying on one of his frequent West Coast jaunts. He barely glanced at it.

A week later, the publishing chief at Knopf called me into his office. He had just had a call from Alistair Cooke. Cooke was furious. He had never been edited like this in his life and he wouldn't stand for it. The book was off.

With my heart in my mouth, I decided I had to go see him, at his apartment on Fifth Avenue. Sitting in his library, with his wall of American books arranged geographically (New England at upper right, California at left, next to the window), I listened to him fulminate. He was flushed with anger. Then, gradually, we got into specifics: particular sections, sentences, words. The atmosphere eased. Sometimes he was right – I had made unnecessary changes. But at least as often he admitted that I had improved things, especially by cutting (the text had been much too long). In the end he agreed to go through the manuscript carefully. A great deal of my editing fortunately stood the test, the book (even more fortunately) was a huge bestseller, and I still use the dictionary he later gave me as a gift, signed 'With affection, Alistair'.

In telling this story I don't mean to brag about my editing skills; I was 20 before I had a clear idea of how to use the word 'hardly', and even older before I grasped the difference between a restrictive and a non-restrictive clause. Use of the subjunctive following 'if' frequently troubles me even now. I learn, as I have said, by doing. I still regret the fact that after writing seventy-five brilliant pages on the comma, an author of mine named Mary Claire Van Leunen gave up her attempt to produce a modern grammar and went to work in IT instead. That is a book I would have loved to publish. Still, I now know quite a lot about commas.

Although a book editor never quite leaves the niceties of line editing behind (especially in the United States, where publishing houses are mostly richer and better staffed, and hence allow more time to be spent on a given title), other activities quickly predominate. When I was hired by Knopf, the first thing I was told was, 'We don't need an editor, we need a publisher.' It took a while to find out that this meant, in essence, finding books that would sell and then doing whatever was necessary to sell them. In practical terms, of course, the process involved a remarkable range of duties, such as understanding contracts, co-opting agents, delivering authoritative statements on libel law and plagiarism, writing copy, comforting sad or disgruntled

Broadaxe or scalpel? By David Eccles

authors, presenting books at sales conferences, and maybe even doing a little line editing. Nothing, in short, that the average literate graduate oughtn't to be well-prepared for.

If all this strikes you as pretty unromantic stuff, you're right. The romance of publishing for editors lies in dealing with authors and their books, not in sorting out reversion clauses. We all – American editors, anyway – remember Maxwell Perkins, our blue-pencil saint, the legendary 1930s Scribner's editor who handled Hemingway and Fitzgerald and created a bestseller out of a mountain of a manuscript by Thomas Wolfe (the *Look Homeward Angel* Wolfe, that is, not the somewhat less logorrhoeic *Bonfire of the Vanities* one). To this day, Perkins's spectre hangs over the publishing scene, justifying an editor's tendency to speak proprietorially of 'his' or 'her' authors.

The relationship between a writer and an editor is probably

mysterious to those who have never experienced it. The best way to think of it may be the relationship between a whale and a pilot fish. Or, more accurately, the relationship between a large, powerful beast like a hippopotamus and the little bird that perches on its head, pecking the insects that would otherwise bother the behemoth. The symbiosis is generally a happy one. If it isn't, the large creature simply twitches, and finds another publisher.

Nevertheless the biggest beast often needs a hand, or a prod. My friend Bob Gottlieb, editor-in-chief of Knopf for many years before taking on the editorship of the *New Yorker*, succeeded against the odds in getting a finished manuscript out of Bill Clinton, only a year or two late. Then there's the well-known story of Sonny Mehta (coincidentally Gottlieb's successor at Knopf) locking the late Douglas Adams into a hotel room for three weeks to get him to finish *So Long and Thanks for All the Fish*. ('I love deadlines,' Adams once remarked. 'I love the whooshing noise they make as they go by.') In my own experience, seriously dilatory authors have never posed much of a problem, partly because Knopf is not as savage in insisting upon delivery dates as some other houses. Even so, performers like the wonderful P. D. James are rare. She tends to surprise us by coming up with a new book even before we expect it.

With most non-fiction contracted for in advance, on the basis of an outline that can be speculative (to put it kindly), delivery schedules may not make much sense anyway. Books change in the writing. On several occasions I have commissioned a single-volume biography that ultimately turned out to be two, and grew from a proposed 150,000 words to a hefty three or four hundred thousand. From a publishing point of view, this is not a happy development; it's tough to market a second volume five years after the first. But who would claim that Janet Browne's magisterial biography of Darwin, to mention only one example, should not have been written in that form? Certainly not me. I don't even begrudge the extra years it took her to write it that way.

My favourite long book never achieved the kind of success I thought it deserved. Maybe it really was too long. Noel Mostert's epic history of the coming together of black and white in South Africa over the course of three hundred years clocked in at 1,355 closely packed pages, every one of them brilliant, scarcely a word superfluous or disposable. I can testify to that, having spent months going carefully through the text in search of places to cut (and seldom finding any). When Mostert began, it was to have been a much smaller book, on a much smaller segment of history, but it rightly grew. I suppose the project might have been aborted; that's what strong editors are supposed to do, no doubt. But I'm glad I didn't. I harbour the fixed hope – as I'm sure Mostert does too – that some day it will be recognized for the masterwork it is.

Besides, sometimes you win. A case in point is Maxine Hong Kingston's *The Woman Warrior*, which dropped unannounced on my desk somewhere around 1975. Although Kingston had never published a word before (except, she admitted, a piece in a children's magazine when she was 12), her manuscript struck me as extraordinary, a mesmerizing mixture of autobiography and fantasy set forth in a hard-edged Chinese-influenced English. We took it on and published a few thousand copies. The total in print by now must be in the millions. One of my happiest memories is of Maxine coming to New York in midwinter from Hawaii, where she was then living, to receive a prestigious National Book Critics Circle award. With no warm clothes to her name, she had borrowed a neighbour's coat and a bobble hat. The problem was that Maxine is about four feet nothing, and the coat was full size. Worse, when she appeared on the podium to respond to the award, she couldn't see over the lectern, and I was convinced that the whole thing would be an embarrassing disaster. I need not have worried – she spoke with enough poise and eloquence to bring tears to the eyes.

Inevitably, an editor's life has its down moments. Rejecting a commissioned book that a writer has spent years on – something I've had to do only once – may be the worst. Attempting to comfort a writer over bad sales is slightly easier, though regrettably common. (It will give you some sense of the pleasant but eccentric atmosphere of the Knopf operation under Gottlieb when I note that we had a running contest to see which book on a given list had the smallest sale. I may be wrong, but I believe that a certain novel that will not be named actually scored in negative numbers, perhaps because of a mix-up calculating returns.) Then there's the author who is determined to self-destruct, taking his book with him, and nothing you can say or do seems to make any difference.

Yet I recall more good moments than bad: David Halberstam, the most fluent writer (and fastest typist) I've known, producing a perfect 250-word patch in minutes for a necessary transition; Dr Meyer Friedman, inventor of the concept of Type A Behaviour (and whose book about it we made a bestseller), assuring me that I was Type B and thus guaranteed not to have a heart attack before 80 (so far so good); Robert Hughes drawing a long, apposite and accurate quote completely from memory to buttress a point in *The Fatal Shore*; Yukio Mishima leading an evening pub crawl through some fairly dark corners of the Tokyo *shitamachi*. You don't have to be Maxwell Perkins to feel that in a small way you have been in closer than average touch with modern civilization. So far as I am concerned, that justifies a lot of years spent restoring split infinitives.

CHARLES ELLIOTT has been an editor for most of his now rather long life. He is the author of several books of essays on gardening and garden history, the latest of which will be published in the autumn this year.

Coming attractions . . .

FRANCES DONNOLLY meets some excellent women

GORDON BOWKER tends a pot plant

MICHELE HANSON takes cold comfort

FRANCES WOOD is driven dotty by the Dewey system

LINDA LEATHERBARROW goes trout-fishing

LAWRENCE SAIL finds the best of all possible worlds

JUSTIN MAROZZI meets Leo the African

URSULA BUCHAN gardens on the margins

WILLIAM PALMER sees ghosts

THE ROYAL SOCIETY OF LITERATURE
LECTURES

Monday, 27 March: Sara Wheeler, 'And so the years passed'.
Chair: Jeremy Lewis

Monday, 24 April: Julian Barnes in conversation with Kate Summerscale,
'An unofficial Englishman'

Monday, 8 May: Bernard MacLaverty, Archie Markham, Helen Simpson,
'Short stories: beginning, middle or end?' Chair: Georgina Hammick

Monday, 5 June: The T. S. Eliot Memorial Reading:
David Harsent and Jo Shapcott, 'Two poets'. Chair: David Dabydeen

The lectures take place in the Kenneth Clark Lecture Theatre, Courtauld Institute, Somerset House, London, and begin punctually at 7 p.m. Members of the public are welcome to attend. The Society suggests a contribution of £5. For details on how to join the Society please call 020 7845 4676.

Bibliography

Rosemary Davidson (ed.), *Gwen Raverat: Wood Engravings of Cambridge and Surroundings* 47

_____ *Gwen Raverat in France* 47

Daniel Defoe, *Robinson Crusoe* 50

Norman F. Dixon, *On the Psychology of Military Incompetence* 11

Percy FitzPatrick, *Jock of the Bushveld* 67

E. H. Gombrich, *A Little History of the World* 55

Elizabeth Anna Hart, *The Runaway* 47

James Hilton, *Lost Horizon* 82

Emanuel Litvinoff, *Journey Through a Small Planet* 63

Fitzroy Maclean, *Eastern Approaches* 35

H. E. Marshall, *Our Island Story* 55

William Pryor (ed.), *Virginia Woolf and the Raverats* 47

Simon Sebag Montefiore, *My Affair with Stalin* 31

Flannery O'Connor, *Wise Blood* 17

Paul Scott, *Staying On* 7

Joanna Selbourne & Lindsay Newman, *Gwen Raverat, Wood Engraver* 47

Frances Spalding, *Gwen Raverat: Friends, Family, Affections* 47

Peter Vansittart, *The Tournament* 71

Evelyn Waugh, *Put Out More Flags* 77